stil warm from the oven.

It's like a piña colada on a plate!

This cake is my mom's favorite.

I'm in love with pure maple syrup.

Warning—there is espresso in here.

es like cream. d a olve.

Don't taste this cake right out of the oven or you'll eat the whole batch!

I had my first tres leches cake in Los Angeles when I worked as a health educator in the San Fernando Valley.

Whether it beverage is always

The salt-and-sugar crust makes these Crunchy Feet taste like margaritas.

This is one of those recipes that hits home with me.

The colors of this cake remind me of a tiger.

es

I created this cake for me—I'm into mace and nutmeg more than the average person.

Somehow this cake tastes like cookies-and-cream ice cream. That's a good thing—and a mystery I don't try to solve.

Hit the holidays in high spirits with this banner cake.

made without a mixer

It may seem unusual to comb with corn, but I was inspired and Aztec traditional beverag chocolate, corn, water, and s

into mace rage person.

Pumpkin is great for baking any time of the year.

Sweet flirts with heat in this orange, mango, and cayenne-pepper cake.

"There's nothing like a little Citron Bundt to start the day!"

It's like ice cream and candy smashed together.

This cake attracts crowds when served, especially w warm from the oven.

rup.

This cake is inspired by the impressive list of indigenous foods from Chiapas, a state

love

cakelove

How to Bake Cakes from Scratch

Warren Brown

photographs by Renée Comet

Stewart, Tabori & Chang

New York

To my parents Beatrice and Leon

Thank you for the immense support, opportunity, and love you have given to me.

With love always,

Warren

Published in 2008 by Stewart, Tabori & Chang
An imprint of Harry N. Abrams, Inc.

Library of Congress Cataloging-in-Publication Data
Brown, Warren, 1970-
   CakeLove : how to bake cakes from scratch / Warren Brown.
      p. cm.
   Includes index.
   ISBN 978-1-58479-662-6
   1. Cake. 2. CakeLove (Bakery) I. Title. II. Title: How to bake cakes from scratch. III. Title:
Cake love.

 TX771.B8785 2008
 641.8'653--dc22
                            2007037543

Editors: Christine Gardner and Jennifer Levesque
Designers: Matthew Bouloutian and Vivian Ghazarian
Production Manager: Tina Cameron
Photo Assistant: Kathryn Norwood
Prop Styling: Audrey Weppler
Props: Sur La Table

The text in this book was composed in Corporate and Leviathan.

Printed and bound in China
10 9 8 7 6 5 4 3 2

HNA
harry n. abrams, inc.
a subsidiary of La Martinière Groupe
115 West 18th Street
New York, NY 10011
www.hnabooks.com

9/08
Rst

CONTENTS

Introduction

This book is a tour of how and why I bake cakes from scratch.

"LCD" Vanilla Pound Cake with Whipped Cream and Sugared Strawberries

"I can cook but I can't bake." That summed up my know-how in the kitchen until I embarked on a New Year's resolution in 1999 to learn how to bake. Until then, I had a complete fear of flour. The baking experience I did have was limited to sweet potato pies baked in store-bought pie shells and boxed-mix pancakes or cornbread. Don't get me wrong—there's nothing wrong with that. Whether it's from scratch or from a box, baking anything at home is better than nothing at all. But when I began baking from scratch I was amazed to see that getting it right wasn't as hard as I thought it would be, and the taste was unbeatable.

Every time someone learns I stopped practicing law to open a bakery, they want to know, "Why cake? What is it about cake that's so compelling?" Well, simply put, it touched me.

Late one Friday night—two years before I opened CakeLove—I was agonizing over how to make a cake look special for one of the senior managers in my office. It was a layered vanilla and almond butter cake with candied navel orange segments and lightly dried orange rind in the buttercream. I took some extra orange segments and put them on the top of the cake in a star-shaped pattern.

To my surprise I was overwhelmed with emotion and memories. The pattern of the orange segments was identical to one I used to draw a lot with oil pastels and colored chalk years before. I also had flashbacks of track practice in sixth grade, biting into cold navel orange segments after running five miles, the farthest I had ever run in my life. There were also thoughts of deceased friends to whom I pray whenever I feel alone. I was exhausted and overwhelmed, and in an instant I lost it and began sobbing over this cake. My past, present, and future suddenly converged and I could see my entire life more clearly than ever before—all because of a cake. My own doubts over whether I should continue baking just disappeared. Cake was it.

As I prepared to open my bakery, baking took on a new role in my life. I felt a mission not just to bake well, but to understand it inside and out. I knew I needed to take the guesswork out of baking from scratch so that every batch matched the one before

it. I got to work and pored over as many sources as I could find and baked every type of cake I could imagine eating. I brought my creations to friends, family, and coworkers. Over time I realized that baking is not just careful measuring and excellent ingredients, it's love too.

Love and baking go hand in hand. Bakers like to create treats they know the recipients will enjoy. They think about whom they're baking for and choose recipes accordingly. And, of course, baking takes time. If I hear about someone rushing through a recipe I think to myself, "Where's the love?" Love is the care that can be tasted long after a cake is out of the oven. You're just not baking if you don't add love.

But there is work behind the love of baking cakes from scratch, and here is where we dive in. Baking cake isn't a cakewalk, but it's not rocket science either. When you start, just read the recipe—don't get ahead of yourself, and have fun. Even if you have had bad luck in the kitchen remember that just about everyone loves dessert, so even flops go over well.

This book is a tour of how and why I bake from scratch. I'm self-taught and enjoy blending traditional and unconventional techniques. I enjoy bringing together different schools of thought when I bake—it makes my time in the kitchen an adventure instead of a chore. Some of the steps I call for might seem odd or extreme, but I do them to get the most out of each ingredient. This is how I bake at home and it's how we bake at CakeLove.

I have refrained from making too many suggestions regarding what flavors to pair together because that's the fun of baking. Mix and match the components from the different chapters to make your own creative combinations. The photographs showcase some of the classic flavors that we make at CakeLove, but this is by no means the limit to what you can create. Have fun and experiment. Baking and assembling cakes might take a little getting used to, but that's totally normal. Just have fun and let the rest take care of itself.

Avoid a Predictable Midlife Crisis

For a while before I started baking, I didn't recognize the disconnect between my daily conscious self and the voice of discontent in my head. I acted happy but I was really torn. I don't know when this started but the conflict seemed normal. I just figured I'd deal with it like everyone else who was moping about in their late twenties: bury it, ignore it, or wait for something to change. But settling started to take a toll. I felt like a bobbing mooring, not going under but also not going anywhere. Even though I knew that I wanted out of practicing law, I didn't know what I should do instead or how to get there. To figure it out I tried looking at my future retrospectively, picturing myself twenty years in the future. I envisioned two possible paths: work hard for twenty years and develop an expertise in law, then pursue the dreams that were already building in my head; or skip the middle-aged agony and get on with my pent-up passions right away. I chose the latter because my gut said, "Who are you kidding—avoid the midlife crisis you can predict! Start baking!"

TEN THINGS YOU CAN BUY TO BE A BETTER BAKER

1. Scale

A scale is the best tool you can get if you want to nail these recipes. Use a scale to weigh butter, sugar, flour, and cocoa powder whenever a recipe calls for more than 2 tablespoons. It's much more accurate than the "scoop-and-level" measuring method.

2. Measuring Spoons and Measuring Cups

If you don't have these you can't measure accurately. Accuracy is important in baking, so be sure you get a set that's accurate and complete. I once saw a "cute" set of heart-shaped measuring spoons in a novelty shop that weren't even close to being accurate. I like stainless steel sets because they're long lasting.

3. Sifter

Totally essential, a sifter breaks up any dry ingredients that pass through it, making them better suited for combining in the batter. Get a crank sifter—trigger sifters don't seem to turn the flour as well or as quickly.

4. Standing Mixer

A standing mixer is a worthwhile investment because it frees you to do other tasks in the kitchen. Handheld mixers can do the job, but you have to hold it in the bowl while it mixes. Baking from scratch is a heck of a lot easier with a standing mixer. They're just too practical to be without if you're going to do a lot of baking.

5. Mixing Bowls

Give yourself plenty of space to work with your ingredients—I often see people struggling through recipes with small bowls. Go big and make it easy on yourself. The right-sized bowl should be able to comfortably handle pre-mixing ingredients before adding them to the standing mixer bowl.

1

2

3

4

5

6. Rasp or Plane Zester

This tool is very handy for zesting citrus to add flavor to batter and buttercream. It's also perfect for grating nutmeg!

7. Candy Thermometer

The majority of the buttercreams I make require a candy thermometer. It's not a good idea to guess the temperature of boiling sugar just by looking at it, as it behaves very differently at certain temperatures, and its properties change very quickly. Some thermometers rest more easily in a saucepan than others, something to take into consideration before purchasing one.

6

7

8. Cake Turntable

If you make more than one layered cake per month, do yourself a favor and pick up a turntable. Assembling a cake is awkward and slow without one. When I first began baking I used a wooden lazy Susan that I bought at a yard sale. It was round and it spun; I thought it would be perfect. Not even close. I think I used it once before I went straight to the cake supply shop. Now assembly is a breeze.

8

9. Rubber and Metal Spatulas

A rubber spatula is great for all sorts of jobs—scraping out a bowl, tossing nuts with sugar syrup, scooping buttercream, and much, much more. Get a heat-resistant one and you can do even more with it. A metal spatula is an indispensable tool that comes in various sizes and styles. I like a wooden-handled, medium-sized offset metal spatula, but try out a few different styles when you visit your kitchen supply shop.

10. Oil and Starch Spray

Pan sprays with a combination of oil and starch are unbeatable for Bundts and brioche pans. You'll avoid the mess of dusting cake pans with flour and tapping it out.

9

10

INGREDIENTS

Selecting excellent, all-natural ingredients is one of the most important steps to successful baking. All-natural ingredients help make every baking episode turn out better. If you're accustomed to using some artificial ingredients, try to eliminate them from your kitchen, especially when baking. The unpleasant aftertaste they leave in the mouth is easily detected and will undermine your efforts.

I like to build recipes in my head before I bake. When I'm thinking about a new cake recipe my mind just wanders, rummaging mentally through the pantry. I've found that thinking outside the box when baking is not only possible, but also a lot of fun.

I like to bake cakes with unusual, even scary, flavors. Wherever possible I try to avoid using oddball ingredients that are difficult to find. But, since a lot of the time I'm reaching for new culinary heights and unexpected flavors, my recipes call for some unusual ingredients. If you can't find them locally, don't fret. Check the Resources (see page 218) in the back of this book. There you'll find the contact information you'll need to order an ingredient online or by phone. That's how we do it at CakeLove.

Unbleached All-Purpose Flour

I have some unusual advice: Don't use cake flour. I use unbleached all-purpose flour for all of the cakes at CakeLove—not cake flour. Over the years I've tried both and I like the flavor, structure, and ease of handling that comes with all-purpose flour. This may seem like a radical decision, so let me explain.

When it comes to flour, the most important difference to note is the gluten content. Achieving a soft texture in a cake begins with keeping the gluten in check since it plays a major role in determining the final texture or "crumb" of the cake. Gluten is a protein found in wheat flours that creates long strands that act like a skeleton for baked goods. Gluten becomes active when wheat flour is combined with liquid and stirred. Too much gluten and the cake can taste tough, chewy, and hard; too little and the cake crumbles, has no body, and can feel airy.

Percentage of Gluten Proteins in Dry Ingredients

INGREDIENTS	PERCENTAGE
Yellow Butter Cake (page 99) (7 ounces all-purpose flour + 2 ounces potato starch)	8.2%
cake flour	7%–8%
pastry flour	9%
all-purpose flour	10.5%

I think it's the gluten that provides a good deal of the mild nutty flavor that makes baked goods taste wholesome. All-purpose flour has a flavor that cake flour and pastry flour just don't seem to offer. All-purpose flour has 10.5% gluten-forming protein versus cake flour (7% to 8%) and pastry flour (9%). That small edge adds a whole lot of flavor.

No matter which flour you use, there are steps you can take to limit excess gluten formation. The most important step is to start with the proper amount of flour. Use a scale and sift the flour directly onto the scale to weigh how much you will need. When I began baking, I scooped and leveled the flour in a cup measure before sifting. Each recipe suggested using a scale but the scoop-and-level method seemed easier and more convenient. But once I used a scale, I never went back. Scooping and leveling compresses flour to the tune of 20% to 30% more than the recipe calls for. And while there is always some wiggle room in a recipe—even with cakes made from scratch—there is not that much.

An unusual way to cut back on the gluten content is to decrease the amount of flour to the bare minimum to maintain structural support, then add a little bulk with pure starch. I love this tactic and use it all the time. It's one of the best tricks I've learned. Potato starch is ideal for this. Adding potato or any starch to flour has the same effect as reducing the protein content, but without removing the flavor. Cakes made with all-purpose flour plus potato starch slice easily and won't crumble; their texture is firm yet giving.

Another method, perhaps the most well-known, is to add enough butter to shorten the length of the gluten strands, which I discuss in the butter section that follows. In addition, gently handling the batter throughout the mixing process is crucial. Even when the flour has been measured properly and the butter content is correct, if a baker is heavy handed when mixing or panning, the batter loses volume and the cake may be tough from the overactivated gluten.

Unsalted Butter

The best-tasting cakes are made with butter. A rich, buttery flavor is the hallmark of a homemade cake. I've never been too concerned over whether a cake is high in fat and sugar—it's cake. Don't skimp on the fat, just eat in moderation. It's supposed to be an indulgence.

Since I started baking I've learned a ton about the role butter plays in cake. It's not just for flavor—it really affects the structure and texture of the cake. Technically speaking, all fats are called shortening in baking. Fat shortens the gluten strands that form when flour is moistened and stirred, resulting in a softer texture or crumb in a cake. Some of my recipes that call for nuts, chocolate, or cream rely on the fat in those ingredients to assist

butter in building the right texture in the cake. But my shortening of choice is always butter because of its flavor and character. I use it just about everywhere.

All of the butter called for in this book is unsalted butter with 82% milk fat. This is the standard butter for baking and cooking and is readily available at every grocery store. I've tried heavier European-style butters with 86% milk fat a few times but found that they're just too heavy for American-style cakes. Always use unsalted butter to maintain control over how much salt is in the cake. Too much salt will ruin any dish, especially a cake.

Extra-Fine Granulated Sugar

When I began baking I doubted whether the size of the sugar crystal mattered. Well it matters—a lot. Please don't make the same mistake I did in the early days unless your intended result is a coarse, dense cake. Look on the label of the sugar package for the granulation. Extra-fine and superfine granulated sugars are the standard for baking for good reason.

I think of a well-made cake batter as this: ingredients floating around a lot of air. The air expands during baking, giving cake its height and contributing to its soft texture. While some air in a cake comes from the carbon dioxide given off by baking

Measuring:
The Key to Successful Baking

My default method for measuring any dry ingredient is by weighing it. It's more accurate, it's usually faster, and it's more practical for ingredients with shapes that won't easily fit into a cup measure, like dried apricots. I'll say it a million times in this book: The most important dry ingredient to measure by weight is flour. If there's only one thing that you take away from reading this, let that be it.

To make life easier, all of the measurements for the major dry ingredients are listed by weight with the volume equivalents in parentheses. Every effort was made to maintain an exact conversion of mass to volume, but in some instances the conversion may not match exactly. This was done to simplify the preparations and won't have a noticeable effect on the cake.

soda or baking powder, the majority comes as a result of sugar crystals pushing air into the soft base of the cake batter—butter in creamed cakes (pound cakes and butter cakes) or eggs (whole, whites, or yolks) in foam cakes.

The right-sized crystal is the key to mixing in the correct amount of air. Ounce for ounce, small crystals do the job better than large crystals because they have more surface area and therefore more sharp edges to aerate the batter. The large crystals common in granulated sugar are simply too big to do the job properly. It's not too difficult to find extra-fine granulated sugar at the grocery store and it's our standard sugar at CakeLove. Alternatively, pulsing granulated sugar in a food processor a few times can also provide the necessary crystal size.

Other Sweeteners

Confectioners' sugar or powdered sugar doesn't have a structure that lends itself to aerating cake batter, but I find lots of uses for it. It's great for increasing the sweetness of cakes or buttercreams, and it's always a lifesaver for dressing up dessert in a jiffy.

I use a lot of dark muscovado, an unprocessed dark brown sugar, to accent many of my buttercreams. Heavy with natural molasses, its aroma and flavor just beat the pants off of regular brown sugar. Place them side by side and take a whiff—it's no contest which is better. Regularly available brown sugar is merely refined white sugar mixed with molasses. There is also a light muscovado that's very good too, but I always lean toward dark muscovado for its unmistakable, intense flavor.

I also enjoy using turbinado, a minimally processed cane sugar with large, golden-colored crystals. It fills a lot of roles for me. It adds flavor and texture in cake batters. It adds bulk and creates turbulence in the creaming stage of a few cake recipes. It's a great option for decorating the exterior of cakes and baked goods to give them a very rustic, freshly baked look. Try sprinkling a pinch into each brioche pan prior to depositing the cake

No Artificial Ingredients

I try to pursue an all-natural lifestyle whenever possible. My mom suffers from multiple chemical sensitivity (MCS), so I'm acutely aware of the huge presence that artificial flavors and chemical preservatives have in our food chain and the havoc they wreak on our bodies. I'm encouraged by the growing number of grocers who provide more all-natural and organic options. Hopefully the greater demand for these foods will expand and producers and consumers alike will benefit from the change. You'll see that everything tastes so much better when it's natural. A lifestyle free of artificial ingredients is not only healthier for our bodies, but also more sustainable for our environment. If you haven't considered it already, let baking be your first step in this direction. Your taste buds will be happy, and your insides too!

It's easy to find most of the ingredients in this book either in the baking aisle at your local grocery store or in a gourmet supply shop. If you need to special order something the Resources in the back of this book (see page 218) will direct you. The good thing about most of the pantry ingredients is that they keep for a long, long time, so you shouldn't have any fear of special ordering. Using the proper ingredients will make a tremendous difference in the quality of your finished product.

batter. (When I'm really letting go, I like to make a turbo-charged version of Crunchy Feet [page 31]. I'll mix 2 tablespoons of turbinado with ¼ teaspoon of kosher salt and a dash of cinnamon or cayenne pepper, and then sprinkle pinches into each brioche pan. The crunchy combination is a real surprise.)

Large Eggs

All of the eggs called for in this book are large eggs, the standard size for baking. You can use white or brown eggs. The only difference I've ever found is that brown eggshells tend to shatter more during cracking, but that just might have been me. Shells happen. After months of fishing for shells with all sorts of tools and my fingers, I found that a measuring spoon works the best. Something about the shape of the spoon seems to create a vacuum that helps hold the shell fragment in place to lift it easily from the bowl.

The recipes often call for separating eggs. The most common method is to crack the egg and move the yolk gently from one shell to another to liberate the yolk from the surrounding egg white. You can also let the white pass between your fingers while holding the yolk but, no matter how you do it, it's important that the white be totally yolk free. The tiniest bit of yolk will prevent

the whites from whipping. Keep your tools squeaky clean, too. Any traces of oil or fat on a dirty wire whip or in a bowl will stop a meringue from forming dead in its tracks.

As for egg temperature, I take my eggs straight from the fridge because I think cold eggs are easier to separate. The yolks in warm eggs tend to cling to the whites, making it difficult to separate them cleanly. But it really comes down to personal preference. If you ever need to use warm eggs, it's best to warm whole eggs by running warm tap water over them for 20 to 30 seconds.

Potato Starch

Potato starch is my secret ingredient. I can't emphasize enough how important it is to keep it stocked in the pantry. It's often overlooked and underreported so it may seem like an odd ingredient. But it's very pure and feels silky between the fingers. It tastes clean, absorbs twice as much moisture as wheat flour, cooks at a lower temperature than cornstarch, and is softer than grain-based starches.

Today potato starch is more commonly available in the specialty baking or ethnic food aisles in the grocery store. Individuals with gluten allergies or celiac disease, an intestinal

Disclaimer—
Nothing Is Fat Free

I like cakes with heaps of butter, sugar, eggs, and flour. And I don't feel guilty about eating them either. In fact, I think I eat less because of that fact. I regularly have to test the product at CakeLove, but I do so in moderation—I also exercise regularly. It's only prudent that we allow for indulging in decadent treats because, let's face it, we usually eat them anyway. Self-control breaks down from time to time—it happens to all of us. Rather than fight clawing urges for delicious sweets, I just accept it and have a small taste. When I indulge my cravings and eat something made from scratch, I am satisfied by the pure, natural flavors I can taste. Eating a slice might make you think you've died and gone to heaven, but it alone won't kill you. So bake from scratch, eat to enjoy, and exercise often.

disorder marked by an inability to process gluten, are always looking for gluten-free alternatives to accommodate their restricted diets.

Do not substitute cornstarch for potato starch. They may look the same and behave in similar ways, but I prefer potato starch for baking. It's lighter than cornstarch, bakes more thoroughly in cake batter, and yields a softer cake.

Vanilla

It's the most popular flavor in the world and we all know why. Baking wouldn't be the same without the sweet, woodsy, warm sensation that vanilla brings to mind. When I was young, my mom put bowls of vanilla all around our house when it was painted, which made the whole place smell like a bakery. I don't know if the vanilla absorbed or just covered the smell of the fresh paint, but I think about it just about every time I pour out a teaspoon of vanilla extract or split a vanilla bean.

There are several options for working vanilla into any recipe: vanilla bean, pure vanilla extract, or vanilla powder. In addition, vanilla is now mass-produced in various tropical climates around the world, so the selection of distinctive vanilla flavors is greater than ever before. Different regions offer different nuances of flavor from woodsy and earthy Mexican to a spicy and floral Tahitian. I prefer garden-variety Madagascar Bourbon vanilla beans and extract for their easily recognizable sweet flavor and plentiful supply.

Plump, ripe vanilla beans offer the best flavor but they're expensive. If you do a lot of baking, try buying them by the pound from a gourmet wholesaler—the savings can be substantial. To remove the seeds from the bean, slice it down the center with a paring knife, then scrape the dull end of the knife down the bean in both directions. These seeds are bursting with flavor so don't miss any! Save the empty pod and use it to flavor brandy or milk by simply dropping it in the bottle.

Pure vanilla extract is perfect for any recipe and much easier to use than the beans. It's perfectly OK to substitute 1 tablespoon of extract for a vanilla bean. Avoid using artificial or imitation vanilla extract. It leaves a noticeable aftertaste and will change the overall flavor of your baking.

Vanilla powder is a great way to add an extra layer of vanilla flavor, but it's not absolutely necessary. I use it to back up the flavor from the bean or extract. Vanilla powder doesn't dominate or play a prominent role; it's more like an extra on a movie set. If you can't find it or don't want to buy it, but you want to intensify the vanilla flavor, simply add 1 to 2 extra teaspoons of vanilla extract.

Fair-Trade Chocolate

Chocolate begins its long path to our kitchens from cacao trees grown in tropical climates. Cacao pods the size of mini-footballs are harvested from the trees. The seeds, or cocoa beans, are fermented, dried, and shipped to manufacturing plants, mostly in Europe and the United States. Recently cocoa cooperatives and independent manufacturers have begun processing chocolate in its country of origin. This helps bring more of the wealth from the chocolate industry back to the farmer and the growing community. Look for fair-trade chocolates when you're shopping to ensure that the farmers have received fair prices for their products.

Chocolate

I'm not a chocoholic by nature, but I've grown to appreciate everything it has to offer. Chocolate is exciting because everyone equates it with indulgence—no matter how minor. One of the best things you can do in the kitchen is to bake with high quality gourmet chocolates. Whether it's chocolate chip cookies or a rich blanket of ganache for a layered cake, when you work with good chocolate everyone will know the difference instantly.

Chocolate is classified into the following types: unsweetened, bittersweet, semisweet, and milk chocolate. Recently chocolatiers have begun marketing more options to indulge our habit, offering chocolates that range from 70% to 85% chocolate mass. These are not the traditional bittersweet varieties, but are mostly for snacking or baking the darkest of fudgey brownies and chunky chocolate cookies. But watch out—the higher the percentage, the more bitter the taste that awaits you. Be prepared for intense flavors if you go over 72%, and save the 100% for brownies only.

The only solid chocolate called for in this book is bittersweet. I think that 60% chocolate mass is the one to select. It's bold, concentrated enough for chocoholics, yet mild enough for those who are wary of chocolate's assertive bite.

Chocolate Mass Percentage

CHOCOLATE MASS PERCENTAGE	TYPE	COLOR
34%	Milk chocolate	Light brown
55%	Semisweet	Medium brown
60%–72%	Bittersweet	Dark brown
80%–99%	Bittersweet	Very dark brown
100%	Unsweetened	Brown-black

Unsweetened Dutch-Processed Cocoa Powder

Winning the battle against dry or dense chocolate cake starts with using a good cocoa powder. Melting solid chocolate is great for brownies as well as for ganache and chocolate glazes to cover a cake, but when it comes to adding chocolate to cake batter, I always use unsweetened, Dutch-processed cocoa powder. All cocoa powder used in baking should be unsweetened, for the same reason butter should always be unsalted. Maintaining control over the quantity of each ingredient is the cornerstone to successful baking from scratch.

Most of the cocoa powder available in grocery stores in the United States is Dutch-processed and has 10%–12% cocoa butter. Dutch-processed cocoa powder is processed with an alkali to reduce the cocoa's natural acidity.

At the bakery I use unsweetened Dutch-processed cocoa powder with 22% to 24% cocoa butter. This tends to be less available in grocery stores, but can be mail ordered (see Resources, page 218). The extra cocoa butter (double the regular amount) works wonders at preventing any chocolate cake from becoming too dry. Cocoa powder with 10%–12% cocoa butter will work perfectly well in all of the recipes in this book.

I've seen recipes that instruct the baker to combine cocoa powder with boiling water before adding it to the batter. I've always had a hard time understanding the sense of this. I just whisk the cocoa powder directly into the other dry ingredients. It's fast. The boiling water routine takes a lot of time—wait for the water to boil, stir into the cocoa powder, then wait for the combination to cool down.... Who has time for that?

Adding water to a cake also runs counter to a fundamental rule in my life, which I like to follow as much as possible, even in the kitchen: Leave something good behind. When water cooks off, nothing is left behind. So if I ever need to use a liquid when baking I'll use milk. If I'm cooking, I'll use stock, wine, or juice.

Other recipes that I have a gripe with call for adding coffee to chocolate cake to enhance the chocolate's flavor. Good chocolate doesn't need help. And, personally, I can't handle the caffeine from coffee and chocolate together.

I also stay away from using melted chocolate in cake batter. If I do use it, the cake always bakes with a heavy crust over the top and has a dense texture. I think there is too much cocoa butter in solid chocolate to provide the light texture that most cakes require. Stick with good cocoa powder—it will make a huge difference in your chocolate cakes.

Dairy Products

People assume that milk is a major ingredient in every cake. I use a lot of milk when baking, but not in cake. It's too thin for my taste and results in a cake texture that is a little dry. Instead I use sour cream, half-and-half, or heavy cream. These ingredients carry their own flavors and enough fat to help manage the gluten proteins in the flour.

Sour cream is ideal for pound cakes because it's thick and slightly tangy. I'm always amazed at how well sour cream blends into the batter and holds everything together. I use tubs and tubs of sour cream in the pound cake section. Don't substitute low-fat or nonfat sour cream for regular sour cream. They tend to have more water than regular versions, and although the cake batter may look right, it won't bake the same.

Half-and-half may seem like an odd choice, but it works wonderfully. In the Chocolate Butter Cake (page 97) and Yellow Butter Cake (page 99), half-and-half provides the perfect balance of fats and liquids for the other ingredients. I have to thank my mom for inspiring me to use half-and-half. For a brief stint she poured it on cereal instead of milk. I tried it once and a bowl of cereal never tasted so good! (It was really rich, though.)

Heavy cream should always be used sparingly in cakes. Its sweet heaviness is ideal for boosting the sticky-dense factor for some pound cakes, but don't go overboard or the finished cake will stick to everything—the pan, your fingers, the plate. A little goes a long way. It can be used for whipped cream, too, if you're ever in a pinch. Whipping cream is a touch lighter than heavy cream and will, therefore, whip better, but heavy cream will work as well—just don't be too aggressive with the wire whip when making whipped cream.

Liqueurs and Other Flavorings

I was telling my friend about the ingredients for Sassy (page 40) and when I got to the liqueurs, she said "Oh, sounds expensive." It doesn't have to be. You can buy the little 50-milliliter bottles for just a couple of dollars and have enough to make several cakes. Bingo! There's a huge difference between stocking the pantry for baking and stocking a bar for a party.

I like to bake with liqueurs because they really create a depth of flavor that is otherwise difficult to achieve. (Even vanilla extract is 36% alcohol.) A little goes a long way. But, you don't have to include liqueurs if you don't want to. To accommodate alcohol-free baking I've included a substitution for each recipe. That way, if you prefer to omit the alcohol, you won't compromise the quality of the cake. There are a lot of alternative flavor sources besides liqueurs that I use all of the time, including alcohol-free vanilla extract, real vanilla bean, gourmet flavored oils, fresh citrus zests, and aromatic spices.

Chocolate
Behind the Scenes

Raw cocoa beans have a rather unpleasant taste and are nothing like the chocolate we're used to eating. Transforming the bitter, rank-tasting cocoa bean into gourmet chocolate or cocoa powder is a long process.

This process begins by letting the cacao pods lightly ferment after being harvested, to develop the flavor of the beans before they are removed, dried, and roasted. Next the shells are removed and the beans are pressed to separate the chocolate liquor (which is brown) from the cocoa butter (which is white). The chocolate you'll see in the market in the form of chocolate chips or baking squares is made by combining chocolate liquor with sugar, cocoa butter, milk solids, flavorings like vanilla, and natural stabilizers, depending on the recipe. Conching—rolling the chocolate in giant machines, sometimes for days—is the final step that makes it ultra-smooth.

The amount of chocolate liquor and cocoa butter, or chocolate mass, in a piece of chocolate is indicated by the percentage count on the label. For legal trade, anything marketed as chocolate must contain chocolate liquor. White chocolate contains cocoa butter, milk solids, sugar, and vanilla, but not chocolate liquor—otherwise it would have some hint of brown in it. It really shouldn't be called chocolate, but the name caught on and everyone continues to use it. For the sake of quality, any chocolate you use should always contain chocolate liquor and cocoa butter. Avoid using chocolates that include vegetable shortening, which is often added in lieu of cocoa butter to reduce manufacturing costs. It makes the chocolate taste greasy and leaves a noticeable residue on the palate.

BAKING IN SPECIAL CONDITIONS

High-Altitude Baking

I find the difference between sea-level and high-altitude recipes interesting. When I'm baking at high altitude (5,000 feet above sea level), these are the basics I review in my head before I crack the first egg:

• **The timing is wacky.** You know what they say about dry heat. Because there's less water vapor in the air to trap and retain the heat, it doesn't feel as hot. At high altitude there is less water vapor, too. There's also much less of the other naturally occurring atmospheric gases—like oxygen—in the air. Without the same quantities of gases to trap and retain the heat as there are at sea level, the air doesn't conduct the oven's heat as effectively. The result is that it takes longer for cakes to bake.

• **The batter might misbehave.** Thinner air also means less pressure on the cake batter as it bakes. Cakes will rise faster with less effort. And rapidly rising batter is vulnerable to collapsing unless we help out by giving the structure a slight boost.

• **The quantities are different.** To help the batter behave better, reduce the baking soda or baking powder and bump up the amount of protein from flour or eggs to make it all work.

• **Get back to sea level as soon as possible!** If your head is swimming, don't worry. I have tried to simplify everything for you by including high-altitude adjustments for each recipe so you can be confident that the results will be delicious.

Baking in High Humidity

Humidity, atmospheric pressure, and temperature always have an effect on baking. Sometimes it's very noticeable, other times it isn't. In the nation's capital it's the humidity that I combat the most. The chocolate butter cakes tend to sink in the center right around mid-May—that's when high humidity and rising summer temperatures become a regular part of our weather report. To adjust, I increase the temperature by a few degrees and bake for a few minutes longer. This effectively burns off the excess moisture in the air that otherwise weighs the cake down and slows the baking.

Serve at Room Temperature

All of the cakes in this book are just like the ones we bake and serve at CakeLove and LoveCafe. So the advice I give about when and how they will taste best really comes from experience. They'll taste better at room temperature. I say that a lot. I'm a freak about this because I'm a freak about taste. Cold butter has much less flavor and a harder, more brittle texture than butter at room temperature. All of that butter in the CakeLove recipes goes right into the CakeLove cakes, so if they're served cold they'll have much less flavor and a harder, more brittle texture than cakes served at room temperature. Not sure? Have a taste test to compare the flavor of cake stored under a cake dome on the counter with cake stored in the fridge—it's a fun project.

Chocolate Pound Cake with Ganache and melted white chocolate

Pound Cakes

One of my fondest memories about cake is eating a 7UP pound cake made from scratch.

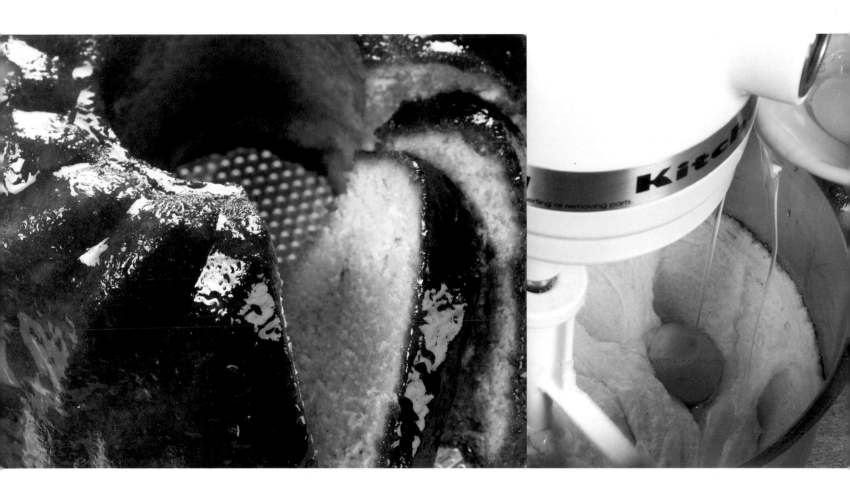

The humble pound cake is the perfect cake for me. It can be eaten in big bites. Its flavors are straightforward. It looks impressive. And, it's easy to bake. One of my fondest memories about cake is eating a 7UP pound cake made from scratch. My mom's friend, Sarah Whitehead, baked it and shared it with my sisters and me when we visited one afternoon. I couldn't believe it tasted so good! I know I had seconds and probably tried to sneak thirds.

While the focus of this chapter is pound cakes, the recipes in the Butter Cakes chapter (page 92) share many of the same directions. The biggest difference is that pound cakes require more ingredients, so the mixing time will be longer. The following section gives step-by-step instructions for mixing both types of cake.

Preheat the oven to 335°F convection or 350°F conventional.
Don't put cake batter into a cold oven. Cake batter is made up of ingredients suspended around pockets of air. Air is one of the most important components of the cake, so catering to its needs at all stages is essential for success. Heat needs to hit the batter from all directions right from the start so that the air trapped in the batter during the mixing process can start expanding.

Place the rack in the middle of the oven. Note, however, that for baking cupcakes at high altitude, racks should be placed on the top and bottom shelves. Every oven behaves a little differently from the next, so the advice given here may not apply to your oven. The main idea is to avoid hot spots in the oven and to separate or provide enough space around the cakes so that the airflow is not blocked, especially in convection ovens, which bake your cake by circulating hot air around it.

Prepare the ingredients and set out the equipment.
Don't start the mixer until all the ingredients are ready for action. The culinary term for this is *mise en place*—everything in its place—and it's a sound practice in the kitchen that helps you to avoid errors. Mistakes happen. It's easy to forget where you are in the recipe once the mixer starts. I have been known to forget to add chocolate chips to the chocolate chip cookie

Starter
Cake

Pound cake was my starter cake. I found the county fair–winning recipe published in the local newspaper and went for it. I baked one for my Grandma Sallie's birthday and brought it to her in Philadelphia, where my family had a party for her on one of those riverboat tours with cheesy singing and dancing

numbers—and we all loved it! She used to make pound cake when she visited. I don't remember watching her bake it, but I sure do remember eating it.

Whenever I teach a class, I always fall back on pound cake because it's almost foolproof, the ingredients are readily available, and it bakes evenly

(especially in a Bundt pan). I also like it because once it's out of the oven, it can be served plain or with minimal finishing touches. Share some of the pound cakes in this book with your friends or coworkers—they'll love you for it!

"LCD" Vanilla Pound Cake ingredients

dough if I'm not careful! So I strongly suggest that you measure the ingredients, place them in prep bowls, and set them aside for use. It takes a little longer, but I do it all of the time because it helps me maintain control over what I'm doing.

Sift the flour and weigh it on a scale.

Notice that I did not say "scoop and level" to measure the flour. Scooping and leveling is a common method for measuring, but I strongly disagree with it. One of the problems I see and taste frequently is too much flour in cake. Since most recipes call for scooping and leveling, I'm inclined to believe that it's responsible for pasty, dense cake. It's really easy to inadvertently compress more flour into the measuring cup than you want with the scoop-and-level technique. In fact, not compressing the flour is almost impossible. If I scoop, level, and then sift, there's 30% more flour in my mixing bowl than if I sifted directly into a bowl placed on a scale.* That's way too much flour and will permanently throw any batter out of balance. Skip all of this fuss, and weigh the ingredients on a scale. I know people resist doing this, but it's the easiest and best thing you can do to improve your baking.

Sifting helps break up the flour, thereby lightening the batter. Some people rely on the manufacturer's promise that sifting isn't necessary because it's done at the factory. Well, they may sift at the factory, but since we're not buying at the factory it's guaranteed to settle during shipping. Please sift.

In the interest of time and accuracy, sift the flour directly into a bowl set on your kitchen scale. If you don't have a scale, please consider buying one. When I did, everything I baked went from average to better than ever.

* This is so important it warrants an asterisk!

To test whether flour compacts during scooping and leveling, I compared two equivalent volume measurements of all-purpose flour and found that their mass was not the same. First I measured out 4 tablespoons, which weighed 24 grams. Next I scooped and leveled ¼ cup, which registered 32 grams—that's a full 30% more, and a serious problem when it comes to baking.

Whisk the ingredients to blend.

Once you've measured the dry and liquid ingredients in separate prep bowls, whisking each for about 10 seconds to blend before introducing them into the batter is very important. This way you're not relying only on the flat paddle to do all of the mixing, which can overwork the batter. If you whisk the dry ingredients first followed by the liquid ingredients, only one whisk gets dirty.

Cream the butter and sugar.

OK, this is a major step. Please give this your careful attention.

Creaming applies to pound cakes and butter cakes and means incorporating air into the butter and sugar. When I started baking I thought it meant to pour heavy cream into the batter! Not quite. In baking lingo, creaming is a way of saying "adding air." It's a total misnomer but has stuck so we have to live with it.

Aerating the batter properly allows it to rise and contributes greatly to a cake's delicate texture. Even though the proportions of sugar and butter change from one recipe to the next, the process remains the same: Combine the room temperature unsalted butter and extra-fine granulated sugar in the bowl of a standing mixer fitted with the paddle attachment on low speed. Sugar pushes and pulls air into the soft butter with each turn of the paddle so going slowly is essential.

Creaming can't be rushed. It can take anywhere from 2 to 5 minutes to get the right amount of air into the butter and sugar combination. The butter should be at room temperature (about 72°F). Let it come to room temperature on it's own—don't microwave it. Cold butter is too hard for sugar to penetrate, but super-soft or heated butter won't provide enough resistance to retain any air. Humidity, altitude, even barometric pressure, all have an effect on how long creaming will take, but temperature has the greatest effect.

Don't set the mixer on too high a speed either. Too much speed beats the air out of the butter and sugar. With my first standing mixer I beat the heck out of the butter and sugar on high speed and couldn't understand what went wrong. The problem was that I went too fast. No air mixed into the combination—it was just flat, mashed butter and sugar. I advise mixing on the lowest setting. It'll seem like it takes forever, but that gives you plenty of time to clean up or prepare another part of the recipe. Once you're more comfortable with the process you can speed it up a bit if you wish, but always keep it under medium speed.

Add the eggs one at a time.

Every baking recipe is standardized so that the volume of egg whites and yolks is equal to that found in large eggs. Keep this in mind when shopping for ingredients or when scavenging for eggs from your neighbors.

Crack each egg into a small prep bowl and remove any shells with a small measuring spoon. Once you begin adding the eggs, the process will move fairly quickly and it's important to focus on the batter. Add the eggs one at a time. Don't beat them ahead of time because waiting for the yolk to break and disperse is an important element in mixing the batter. Sometimes the yolk slides around the beater without breaking—that's OK. Once the yolk is broken and blended in, add the next egg or yolk.

Scraping down the sides of the bowl after adding the eggs may be necessary. There is usually a lot of butter and sugar stuck to the sides of the bowl. When you scrape the sides, notice the difference in color between the almost white batter stuck to the sides and the yellowish, eggy mix in the middle of the bowl. Scraping after adding the eggs helps avoid overbeating in the next steps.

Alternate adding the dry and liquid ingredients.

When adding ingredients to the batter, it's best to start and end with the dry ingredients. It's not a problem if you accidentally

Dancing   Clumping   Coating

Stages of Creaming

Creaming is a baker's verb for slowly combining sugar and butter for the purpose of driving air into the base of the cake batter. It's the first step in most pound cakes and butter cakes and it can be confusing. Cake batter is really just a bunch of ingredients suspended around air bubbles, so the process of aerating the batter is very important.

Follow these visual cues through the three stages of creaming:

Dancing—The butter and sugar slide loosely around the bowl without combining, almost like they're trying to avoid each other.

Clumping—Both ingredients clump together on the beater in large chunks and stay away from the sides of the bowl.

Coating—The mass falls away from the beater and coats the lower portion of the bowl. The mixture will be white with a fluffy, slightly grainy texture, and the volume of the butter and sugar will have increased due to the incorporation of air.

start with the liquid ingredients or lose track of what ingredient was last added. What matters is to watch carefully for overmixing. It's important to neither overwhelm nor underwhelm the batter with the ingredients. Add just enough ingredients so the batter can absorb them without too much effort—about 4 to 5 revolutions of the mixer's paddle. To get it right you'll really have to watch the batter because it changes constantly. Add about ½ cup of the dry ingredients in 2 to 3 scoops followed by about

a third of the liquid ingredients. As soon as the liquid ingredients are blended in, add the next few scoops of dry ingredients, and so on. It should take about 60 seconds to complete this series of steps. Look around to make sure all of your prep bowls are empty. Once you're sure everything has been added, turn off the mixer and scrape down the bowl with a rubber spatula. Mix on medium speed for the final mix of 20 to 60 seconds, or as indicated by the recipe.

Cream the butter and sugar

Add the eggs

Scrape the sides of the bowl

Alternate dry and liquid ingredients

Scrape again and mix to combine

Spray the cake pan

Deposit the batter

Prepare the pans.

Bundt pans, or brioche pans for Crunchy Feet (page 31), should always be evenly coated with nonstick spray. Pan sprays will save you time and trouble when trying to remove the cake from the pan. Spray evenly in a side-to-side motion to hit all of the crevices. I strongly recommend using a spray that contains a combination of oil and starch instead of just oil. And I'd advise against using butter and dusting the pan with flour—that makes a complete mess.

A lot of bakeware is nonstick, but I prefer aluminum pans. Nonstick bakeware denies the cake a surface against which the sugars can cling to. The sugars then connect with one another, sometimes creating a very tough exterior on the cake. I've noticed this repeatedly in nonstick brioche pans when baking Bundts. Every specialty shaped pan with lots of crevices requires a heavy dose of nonstick spray. You can also drop in a little extra sugar and some nuts to create an exciting streusel topping for your favorite Bundt cake.

Deposit the batter into the pan in three spots to help ensure an even distribution. I always try to deposit the batter roughly at the end points of the shape of the letter Y. When I can remember to do this, it works wonderfully. If you forget, don't worry about it. The batter will slide into place once the pan is in the oven.

Check for doneness.

Always check the bake times for each recipe. In addition, looking for color cues can be helpful but somewhat confusing because the cues can change from batter to batter. In general, blonde batters will have golden-brown edges and creamy-colored or browned tops; a chocolate batter will develop an even brown color across the top. I prefer to judge by appearance. The top of the cake should appear smooth and not liquid. It won't glisten when the oven light is turned on. Also, it won't jiggle when the pan is moved or bumped. Finally, gently insert a wooden skewer into the center of the cake when the color looks right and it's not jiggling. Remove the cake from the oven when the skewer comes out clean or with just a few crumbs on it.

Both amateur and professional pastry chefs tell me that they don't smell the item they're baking until it's just about done. It happens to me, too, even at the bakery where we're baking all day. Customers will walk into the bakery and remark on the glorious smell of the chocolate cake that's in the oven, but I can't smell it. Not until it's about a minute away from being done does the smell hit me. I can't explain it, but it happens all the time!

Remove the cake from the oven.

A freshly baked, hot cake is very delicate. I put my cake pans or cake on a cooling rack if I have one available, but it's not necessary. Placing a hot cake pan on any heat-resistant surface is fine.

Let 9-x-2-inch cake rounds, Bundt cakes, and cupcakes cool until the pans can be handled with bare hands and then remove them. Crunchy Feet should be removed from their pans while they are still quite warm, no more than 5 minutes after removing from the oven. If they cool too long in the pan, they will stick.

All cakes should be thoroughly cooled to room temperature before wrapping in plastic, otherwise condensation will form and ruin the texture of the cake.

Pound Cake Recipe Comparison

The chart below illustrates the notable differences between a traditional pound cake recipe and my recipe. My sugar-to-flour ratio is often the inverse of what some recipes call for. I've tasted many pound cakes and they're usually burdened with too much flour, so the flavor comes out pasty, and with too little sugar so the crumb is too tight. Increasing the amount of sugar and pulling back on the amount of flour are steps in the right direction to achieve the texture I enjoy.

RECIPE	UNSALTED BUTTER	EXTRA-FINE GRANULATED SUGAR	LARGE EGGS	UNBLEACHED ALL-PURPOSE FLOUR	LIQUID	FLAVORINGS
Traditional Fatally flawed with more flour than sugar.	8 ounces (2 sticks).	16 ounces (2 cups). Insufficient for adequate creaming. Final crumb is tight.	6 eggs. Probably a tad more than necessary.	15 ounces (3 cups). Too much. Promises a doughy, tough texture that will taste pasty.	1 cup sour cream. A standard amount. Without extra flavorings the cake will taste bland.	Up to ⅓ cup mixed liqueurs or fresh fruit juices.
LCD My basic pound cake. Dense, creamy, and soft to the bite.	8 ounces (2 sticks). Add the seeds of 1 vanilla bean to enhance the flavor.	24 ounces (3 cups). Better creaming, much better flavor. May taste sweet; can pull back by ¼ cup if desired.	5 eggs, 1 yolk. Dropping 1 egg white enhances density.	13½ ounces (2½ cups + 3 tablespoons) + 1 tablespoon potato starch. Swapping potato starch for some flour lightens the texture.	1 cup sour cream + ¼ cup heavy cream. Adds sweetness and density.	4 tablespoons brandy plus other liqueurs. Increases flavor complexity.

What Are Crunchy Feet?

Crunchy Feet are little pound cakes baked in small (2-ounce) brioche pans. They are so named because they have lots of toes, or ruffled edges, that get a little crunchy when they bake. When I turned out a whole bunch of them on a table, they looked like little creatures that would scurry around. Thus the name "Crunchy Feet" was born. It's an odd stretch, I know, but this is baking after all—we're having fun.

When I was experimenting with Bundt cakes in the early days while I still practiced law, Crunchy Feet were the tester cakes for the actual Bundt. Baking the tester in a brioche pan helped me understand how the cake tasted and whether the structure was too tough or too weak. I was making up recipes for the first time back then and was really unsure of the outcome of each one so I needed a test cake. The brioche pan was ideal because it baked quickly and showed me whether the center of the cake would collapse. If it collapsed, the batter had either too much fat or too little flour.

As I continued to bake and use the test cakes, I realized that they were fun to serve and really cute. It also came to my attention that plenty of people like cake, but not frosting. Satisfaction in one bite became my next goal for Crunchy Feet. Innovative flavors and crazy names to make them inviting got the best of me and soon I was mixing mango, orange, and cayenne pepper into one batter (Sassy, page 40), or ginger, lime, molasses, and honey in another one (Gingerly, page 85). I kept going, and found the whole idea of unusually flavored pound cakes a blast. They're fragile when they're warm, though, so be careful not to break off any toes when removing them from the pans.

That's Crunchy Feet. Utilitarian, kind of random, and baked expressly for people who love cake without frosting.

"LCD" Vanilla Pound Cake

> *This cake is my mom's favorite.*

This cake is my mom's favorite. Once I showed up to visit without anything from the bakery and she said, "Where's the cake?" Now it's a standard part of my luggage for any trip home. I call it "LCD" for lowest common denominator. It's the one pound cake everyone knows and loves.

While this recipe might seem like it has a lot of sugar, it's necessary to drive the right amount of air into the butter during the creaming stage. That air is critical to achieving a textural harmony between light and dense.

The concentration of flavors found here comes from three sources—real vanilla bean, vanilla powder, and vanilla extract. I like this three-pronged approach because it results in a layered composition of flavors. Vanilla powder is available at most gourmet stores, but even without it this cake will still win compliments. Serve plain or as a base for any shortcake. It's an all-time favorite that must not be missed.

EQUIPMENT: mixing bowls, standing mixer, one 12-cup Bundt pan or small brioche pans
YIELD: one 12-cup Bundt cake or 32 Crunchy Feet

"LCD" Vanilla Pound Cake with Apricot Preserve Glaze

INGREDIENTS

Dry

unbleached all-purpose flour
13½ ounces (2½ cups + 3 tablespoons),
or 14½ ounces (2¾ cups + 2 tablespoons)
at high altitude

potato starch, 1 tablespoon

vanilla powder, 1½ teaspoons

salt, ½ teaspoon

baking soda, ¼ teaspoon

Liquid

sour cream, 8 ounces (1 cup)

heavy cream, 2 tablespoons, *or 2 tablespoons*
+ 1 teaspoon at high altitude

brandy, ¼ cup

amaretto, 1 tablespoon

rum, 1 tablespoon

vanilla extract, 1½ teaspoons

whiskey, 1½ teaspoons

Creaming

unsalted butter, at room temperature,
8 ounces (2 sticks)

extra-fine granulated sugar, 24 ounces
(3 cups), *or 21 ounces (2½ cups +*
2 tablespoons) at high altitude

eggs (large), 5, *or 6 at high altitude*

yolk (large), 1

vanilla bean, 1

Alcohol-free variation: Omit the brandy, amaretto, rum, vanilla extract, and whiskey. Substitute 2 tablespoons grated or minced lemon zest and 7 tablespoons whole milk. Whisk to combine with the liquid ingredients.

1. Preheat the oven to 350°F (conventional) or 335°F (convection). Set the rack in the middle of the oven. For Crunchy Feet, set racks in the upper-middle and lower-middle positions.

2. Set out the ingredients and equipment.

• Sift the flour directly into a bowl on a scale for accurate measuring.

• Measure the other dry ingredients into a separate mixing bowl, add the flour, and whisk for 10 seconds to blend. Set aside.

• Measure the liquid ingredients into a separate bowl, whisk to combine, and set aside.

• Measure the butter and sugar into separate bowls and set aside.

• Crack the eggs and yolk into separate bowls and set aside.

3. In the bowl of a standing mixer fitted with the paddle attachment, cream together the butter and sugar on the lowest speed for 2 to 3 minutes.

4. Meanwhile, slice the vanilla bean lengthwise with a paring knife and scrape out the seeds. Add the seeds to the creaming butter and sugar. Reserve the pod for another use.

5. With the mixer still on the lowest speed, add the eggs one at a time followed by the yolk, fully incorporating after each addition. Stop the mixer and scrape the sides of the bowl.

6. Add the dry ingredient mixture alternately with the liquid mixture in 3 to 5 additions each, beginning and ending with the dry mixture. Move swiftly to avoid overworking the batter. Don't wait for the dry or liquid mixtures to be fully incorporated before adding the next. This step should take a total of about 60 seconds.

7. Stop the mixer and scrape the sides of the bowl all the way down. Don't miss the clumps of ingredients hiding on the bottom of the bowl. Mix on medium speed for 15 to 20 seconds to develop the batter's structure.

8. Prepare the pans. For a Bundt cake, spray the pan well with a nonstick spray. For Crunchy Feet, place the brioche pans on sheet pans (16 per half-sheet pan is a snug fit) and spray them liberally.

9. For a Bundt cake, fill the pan about three-quarters full by depositing the batter with the rubber spatula in small clumps around the prepared pan instead of by pouring it into one spot. Level the batter with the rubber spatula. Bake any leftover batter as Crunchy Feet or cupcakes. For Crunchy Feet, use a 2-ounce, trigger-release, ice-cream scoop to deposit the batter into the prepared pans so they're three-quarters full.

10. Follow the approximate bake times listed below.

ITEM	SEA LEVEL	HIGH ALTITUDE
12-cup Bundt	50–55 minutes	70 minutes
Crunchy Feet	15 minutes	30 minutes

11. Once the top of the cake doesn't jiggle in the center, test for doneness by inserting a bamboo skewer in the center of the cake. When the skewer shows just a touch of crumbs the cake is done. The sheen on top may look liquid, but this is normal and comes from the fat in the heavy cream. Remove the pan from the oven and place on a heat-resistant surface or wire rack.

12. For Crunchy Feet, carefully invert the brioche pans to release the cakes 3 to 4 minutes after removing them from the oven—well before they cool completely. You may have to tap each pan firmly—or even slam it—against the sheet pan to release the cake. Place on a heat-resistant surface or wire rack to cool. Immediately soak the pans to make cleaning easier.

13. For the Bundt cake, once the cake has cooled for 5 to 10 minutes remove the cake by inverting the pan onto a flat surface. Allow it to cool to room temperature, about 30 minutes, before glazing.

SERVING AND STORING

Serve at room temperature either naked or with a dusting of confectioners' sugar. To boost flavor and add a special touch, use a fruit preserve glaze from the Frostings and Glazes chapter (page 176) or Glazing Chocolate (page 174).

Store under a cake dome at room temperature, or wrapped in plastic in the fridge for up to 1 week. To store longer, label, date, and store the plastic-wrapped cake in the freezer for up to 1 month.

What To Do with Empty Vanilla Bean Pods

What's the best use for vanilla bean pods after the seeds have been scraped out? Try infusing the richly flavored pods into a liquid. I like to add my empty pods directly into cream before simmering it when making ganache. Or I'll drop one right into a bottle of brandy. I don't put the pods into granulated sugar as is often recommended—the flavor doesn't migrate as easily from crystal to crystal as it would in a liquid.

Chocolate Pound Cake with Ganache

Chocolate Pound Cake

This cake is a trusted standby for chocolate lovers. The taste is simple, it's familiar, and the chocolate flavor is just rich enough. Slices of this cake are even more delicious lightly buttered and warmed in a frying pan. Happy baking!

This recipe makes a lot of batter. You may even have to use two sheet pans and two oven racks to bake 32 Crunchy Feet at the same time.

EQUIPMENT: mixing bowls, standing mixer, one 12-cup Bundt pan or small brioche pans

YIELD: one 12-cup Bundt cake or 32 Crunchy Feet

INGREDIENTS
Dry

unbleached all-purpose flour, 10 ounces (2 cups), or *11 ounces (2¼ cups + 2 tablespoons) at high altitude*

unsweetened cocoa powder, 2 ounces (½ cup + 2 teaspoons), or *2¼ ounces (½ cup + 3 tablespoons) at high altitude*

turbinado sugar, 2 tablespoons

potato starch, 1 teaspoon

vanilla powder, ¼ teaspoon

baking soda, ¼ teaspoon

salt, ¾ teaspoon

Liquid

sour cream, 4 ounces (½ cup)

whole milk, ¾ cup, or *¾ cup + 2 tablespoons at high altitude*

brandy, 2 tablespoons

vanilla extract, 1 teaspoon

Creaming

unsalted butter, at room temperature, 8 ounces (2 sticks)

extra-fine granulated sugar, 24 ounces (3 cups), or *21 ounces (2¾ cups + 2 teaspoons) at high altitude*

eggs (large), 4, or *5 at high altitude*

yolks (large), 3

The Secret to the Best Chocolate Cake

At CakeLove we always use unsweetened cocoa powder in our chocolate cakes. Melted solid chocolate is great for brownies, but I stopped using melted chocolate in my cakes within the first few months of baking because it's too heavy for cake. Every batch I baked with melted chocolate had a heavy, thick crust that was totally unappealing. Instead of adding melted unsweetened solid chocolate to the batter, I combine the cocoa powder with the dry ingredients. It gives me a great chocolate flavor and a rich but light, moist texture.

The commonly available unsweetened cocoa powder has 10% to 12% cocoa butter, which is alright but it also may be a little dry and dull. In my experience, there seems to be something in the chocolate liquor, the flavor-rich brown part of chocolate, that just doesn't bond with other fats as well as it does with cocoa butter. Bumping up the quantity of dairy butter isn't enough, adding cream makes the cake sticky, and vegetable oil merely coats everything in its path, making it feel moist when it's really just greasy. I've fiddled with chocolate cakes for years and still haven't found anything that works quite as well as unsweetened cocoa powder, with 22% to 24% cocoa butter.

Alcohol-free variation: Omit the brandy and vanilla extract. Substitute the seeds from 1 vanilla bean and 2 additional tablespoons whole milk. Whisk to combine with the liquid ingredients.

1. Preheat the oven to 350°F (conventional) or 335°F (convection). Set the rack in the middle of the oven. For Crunchy Feet, set racks in the upper-middle and lower-middle positions.

2. Set out the ingredients and equipment.

• Sift the flour directly into a bowl on a scale for accurate measuring.

• Measure the other dry ingredients into a separate mixing bowl, add the flour, and whisk for 10 seconds to blend. Set aside.

• Measure the liquid ingredients into a separate bowl, whisk to combine, and set aside.

• Measure the butter and sugar into separate bowls and set aside.

• Crack the eggs and yolk into separate bowls and set aside.

3. In the bowl of a standing mixer fitted with the paddle attachment, cream together the butter and sugar on the lowest speed for 2 to 3 minutes.

4. With the mixer still on the lowest speed, add the eggs one at a time followed by the yolk, fully incorporating after each addition. Stop the mixer and scrape the sides of the bowl.

5. Add the dry ingredient mixture alternately with the liquid mixture in 3 to 5 additions each, beginning and ending with the dry mixture. Move swiftly through this step to avoid overworking the batter. Don't wait for the dry or liquid mixtures to be fully incorporated before adding the next. This step should take a total of about 60 seconds.

6. Stop the mixer and scrape the sides of the bowl all the way down. Don't miss the clumps of ingredients hiding on the bottom of the bowl. Mix on medium speed for 15 to 20 seconds to develop the batter's structure.

7. Prepare the pans. For a Bundt cake, spray the pan well with a nonstick spray. For Crunchy Feet, place the brioche pans on sheet pans (16 per half-sheet pan is a snug fit) and spray them liberally.

8. For a Bundt cake, fill the pan about three-quarters full by depositing the batter with the rubber spatula in small clumps around the prepared pan instead of by pouring it into one spot. Level the batter with the rubber spatula. Bake any leftover batter as Crunchy Feet or cupcakes. For Crunchy Feet, use a 2-ounce, trigger-release, ice-cream scoop to deposit the batter into the prepared pans so they're three-quarters full.

9. Follow the approximate bake times listed below.

ITEM	SEA LEVEL	HIGH ALTITUDE
12-cup Bundt	50–55 minutes	60 minutes
Crunchy Feet	15 minutes	32 minutes

10. Once the top of the cake doesn't jiggle in the center, test for doneness by inserting a bamboo skewer in the center of the cake. When the skewer shows just a touch of crumbs or comes out clean, and the color is an even medium brown, the cake is done. Remove the pan from the oven and place on a heat-resistant surface or wire rack.

11. For Crunchy Feet, carefully invert the brioche pans to release the cakes 3 to 4 minutes after removing them from the oven—well before they cool completely. You may have to tap each pan firmly—or even slam it—against the sheet pan to release the cake. Place on a heat-resistant surface or wire rack to cool. Immediately soak the pans to make cleaning easier.

12. For the Bundt cake, once the cake has cooled for 5 to 10 minutes, remove the cake by inverting the pan onto a flat surface. Allow it to cool to room temperature, about 30 minutes, before glazing.

SERVING AND STORING

Serve at room temperature naked or with a dusting of confectioners' sugar. Or use a fruit preserve glaze from the Frostings and Glazes chapter (page 176). For something even richer, serve covered with Ganache (page 172), as on page 36.

Store under a cake dome at room temperature, or wrapped in plastic in the fridge for up to 1 week. To store longer, label, date, and store the plastic-wrapped cake in the freezer for up to 1 month.

Sassy

> *Sweet flirts with heat in this orange, mango, and cayenne-pepper cake.*

Sassy is the most popular flavor of Crunchy Feet at CakeLove! It's one of those wonderful cakes that keeps winning people over every day.

The inspiration for Sassy came to me well before I began baking. I read a book on Malaysian cooking that had a story about a woman who was pounding chile peppers in a mortar and pestle for a thick curry paste. When some of the chile splattered into her eye she was immobilized with pain. Yikes! Her grandfather immediately made a paste of sugar and water to apply to her eye. The searing heat went away and she recovered. Well, since then, I've been intrigued by the power that sugar has to tame pepper. Once I began baking, I thought a cake would be a good place to experiment.

Be sure to use pure orange oil in this recipe. Some brands are a blend of citrus and safflower oils—avoid 'em. They smell great but their flavor isn't as suitable for cakes as the pure oil.

EQUIPMENT: rasp or plane zester, 2-quart heavy-bottomed saucepan, food processor, mixing bowls, standing mixer, one 12-cup Bundt pan or small brioche pans

YIELD: one 12-cup Bundt cake or 32 Crunchy Feet

INGREDIENTS

Dry

unbleached all-purpose flour, 11 ounces
   (2¼ cups + 2 tablespoons), *or 11½ ounces*
   (2 cups + 6 tablespoons) at high altitude

potato starch, 1 tablespoon

salt, ¾ teaspoon

baking soda, ¼ teaspoon

ground cayenne pepper, ¼ teaspoon

Liquid

Mango Puree (page 43), ½ cup

sour cream, 8 ounces (1 cup)

tequila, 2 teaspoons

orange liqueur, 2 teaspoons

lemon liqueur, 2 teaspoons

dark rum, 1 teaspoon

vanilla extract, 1 teaspoon

pure orange oil, ½ teaspoon

Creaming

unsalted butter, at room temperature,
   6 ounces (1½ sticks)

extra-fine granulated sugar, 21 ounces
   (2½ cups + 2 tablespoons), *or 19¾ ounces*
   (2¼ cups + 3 tablespoons) at high altitude

orange zest, 1 tablespoon

eggs (large), 5, *or 6 at high altitude*

yolks (large), 2

Sassy filled with orange-flavored Italian Meringue Buttercream and sprinkled with confectioners' sugar

Alcohol-free variation: Omit the tequila, orange and lemon liqueurs, dark rum, and vanilla extract. Substitute 2 tablespoons freshly squeezed orange juice. Whisk to combine with the liquid ingredients.

PREPARE AHEAD OF TIME

1. Zest the orange with a rasp or mince the orange zest with a chef's knife.

2. Make the Mango Puree (facing page).

1. Preheat the oven to 350°F (conventional) or 335°F (convection). Set the rack in the middle of the oven. For Crunchy Feet, set racks in the upper-middle and lower-middle positions.

2. Set out the ingredients and equipment.

• Sift the flour directly into a bowl on a scale for accurate measuring.

• Measure the other dry ingredients into a separate mixing bowl, add the flour, and whisk for 10 seconds to blend. Set aside.

• Measure the liquid ingredients into a separate bowl, whisk to combine, and set aside.

• Measure the butter and sugar into separate bowls and set aside.

• Crack the eggs and two yolks into two separate bowls and set aside.

3. In the bowl of a standing mixer fitted with the paddle attachment, cream together the butter, sugar, and orange zest on the lowest speed for 3 to 4 minutes. The acids from the orange zest will break down the sugar and the creamed mixture will appear a little wet.

4. With the mixer still on the lowest speed, add the eggs one at a time followed by the two yolks, fully incorporating after each addition. Stop the mixer and scrape the sides of the bowl.

5. Add the dry ingredient mixture alternately with the liquid mixture in 3 to 5 additions each, beginning and ending with the dry mixture. Move swiftly through this step to avoid overworking the batter. Don't wait for the dry or liquid mixtures to be fully

incorporated before adding the next. This step should take a total of about 60 seconds.

6. Stop the mixer and scrape the sides of the bowl all the way down. Don't miss the clumps of ingredients hiding on the bottom of the bowl. Mix on medium speed for 15 to 20 seconds to develop the batter's structure.

7. Prepare the pans. For a Bundt cake, spray the pan well with a nonstick spray. For Crunchy Feet, place the brioche pans on sheet pans (16 per half-sheet pan is a snug fit) and spray them liberally with a nonstick spray.

8. For a Bundt cake, fill the pan about three-quarters full by depositing the batter with the rubber spatula in small clumps around the prepared pan instead of by pouring it into one spot. Level the batter with the rubber spatula. Bake any leftover batter as Crunchy Feet or cupcakes. For Crunchy Feet, use a 2-ounce, trigger-release, ice-cream scoop to deposit the batter into the prepared pans so they're three-quarters full.

9. Follow the approximate bake times listed below.

ITEM	SEA LEVEL	HIGH ALTITUDE
12-cup Bundt	50–55 minutes	55 minutes
Crunchy Feet	15 minutes	32–37 minutes

10. Once the top of the cake doesn't jiggle in the center, test for doneness by inserting a bamboo skewer in the center of the cake. When the skewer shows just a touch of crumbs or comes out clean and the cake is a light gold color on top and browned around the edges, the cake is done. Remove the pan from the oven and place on a heat-resistant surface or wire rack.

11. For Crunchy Feet, carefully invert the brioche pans to release the cakes 3 to 4 minutes after removing them from the oven—well before they cool completely. You may have to tap each pan firmly—or even slam it—against the sheet pan to release the cake. Place on a heat-resistant surface or wire rack to cool. Immediately soak the pans to make cleaning easier.

12. For the Bundt cake, once the cake has cooled for 5 to 10 minutes, remove the cake by inverting the pan onto a flat surface. Allow it to cool to room temperature, about 30 minutes, before glazing.

SERVING AND STORING

Serve at room temperature either naked or with a dusting of confectioners' sugar. To boost flavor and add a beautiful glow, use Apricot Preserve Glaze (page 176). For extra decadence, I like to serve this cake sliced into two layers separated by orange-flavored Italian Meringue Buttercream (page 151) and sprinkled with sugar, as on page 41, or accented with long strips of orange zest.

Store under a cake dome at room temperature, or wrapped in plastic in the fridge for up to 1 week. If frosted, store under a cake dome for up to 3 days, or in the fridge for up to 1 week. To store unfrosted cake longer, label, date, and store the plastic-wrapped cake in the freezer for up to 1 month.

Mango Puree

This recipe can be made with fresh or frozen mango chunks. Ripe mangoes will smell sweet and feel soft—color is not indicative of ripeness. Place mangoes in a brown paper bag with a banana for 1 or 2 days to accelerate ripening.

EQUIPMENT: 2-quart, heavy-bottomed saucepan, food processor
YIELD: about ½ cup

Ingredients

ripe mango, 1
extra-fine granulated sugar, 2 ounces (¼ cup)

1. Cut the flesh of the mango into even-sized pieces and combine with sugar in a 2-quart, heavy-bottomed saucepan.

2. Bring the mixture to a gentle simmer over low to medium heat and cook for 3 minutes. Remove from the heat and allow to cool for 15 minutes. Strain the syrup and reserve for another use.

3. Place the cooked fruit in the bowl of a food processor and puree until totally smooth, about 1 minute.

4. Transfer the puree to an airtight container. Label, date, and store it in the refrigerator for up to 10 days. Better yet, share with a friend for a yummy snack.

Espresso Pound Cake

Warning—there is real espresso in here!

"Tastes like a latte!" my sister Liz said with a big grin when she sampled this cake just hours after the first batch came out of the oven. Bingo? I think so—my goal here was to make a coffee-flavored coffee cake.

I created this recipe on the fly during an early-morning television shoot chronicling my adventures in baking. The producer asked me to create something special. Happy to oblige, I went for a flavor that I was craving that morning: espresso. For the jolt of a double shot, use 8 tablespoons of espresso instead of 6 for a single shot. Warning—this is real espresso in here!

EQUIPMENT: mixing bowls, standing mixer, one 12-cup Bundt pan or small brioche pans

YIELD: one 12-cup Bundt cake or 32 Crunchy Feet

INGREDIENTS

Dry

unbleached all-purpose flour, 12 ounces
   (2¼ cups + 2 tablespoons), *or 12½ ounces*
   (2½ cups) at high altitude

potato starch, 2 tablespoons

vanilla powder, 2 tablespoons

baking soda, ¼ teaspoon

salt, ½ teaspoon

freshly ground espresso (finest grind),
   6 tablespoons

Liquid

sour cream, 6 ounces (¾ cup)

heavy cream, 2 tablespoons, *or 2 tablespoons*
   + 1 teaspoon at high altitude

vanilla extract, 1 teaspoon

brandy, 3 tablespoons

Creaming

unsalted butter, at room temperature,
   6 ounces (1½ sticks)

extra-fine granulated sugar, 16 ounces
   (2 cups), *or 15 ounces at high altitude*

turbinado sugar, 3 tablespoons

eggs (large), 5, *or 6 at high altitude*

Alcohol-free variation: Omit the brandy and vanilla extract and substitute ¼ cup whole milk.

1. Preheat the oven to 350°F (conventional) or 335°F (convection). Set the rack in the middle of the oven. For Crunchy Feet, set racks in the upper-middle and lower-middle positions.

2. Set out the ingredients and equipment.

• Sift the flour directly into a bowl on a scale for accurate measuring.

• Measure the other dry ingredients into a separate mixing bowl, add the flour, and whisk for 10 seconds to blend. Set aside.

• Measure the liquid ingredients into a separate bowl, whisk to combine, and set aside.

• Measure the butter, granulated sugar, and turbinado sugar into separate bowls and set aside.

• Crack the eggs into a separate bowl and set aside.

3. In the bowl of a standing mixer fitted with the paddle attachment, cream together the butter and sugar on the lowest speed for 2 to 3 minutes.

4. With the mixer still on the lowest speed, add the eggs one at a time followed by the yolk, fully incorporating after each addition. Stop the mixer and scrape the sides of the bowl.

5. Add the dry ingredient mixture alternately with the liquid mixture in 3 to 5 additions each, beginning and ending with the dry mixture. Move swiftly through this step to avoid overworking the batter. Don't wait for the dry or liquid mixtures to be fully incorporated before adding the next. This step should take a total of about 60 seconds.

6. Stop the mixer and scrape the sides of the bowl all the way down. Mix on medium speed for 15 to 20 seconds to develop the batter's structure.

7. Prepare the pans. For a Bundt cake, spray the pan well with a nonstick spray. For Crunchy Feet, place the brioche pans on sheet pans (16 per half-sheet pan is a snug fit) and spray them liberally.

8. For a Bundt cake, fill the pan about three-quarters full by depositing the batter with the rubber spatula in small clumps around the prepared pan instead of by pouring it into one spot. Level the batter with the rubber spatula. Bake any leftover batter as Crunchy Feet or cupcakes. For Crunchy Feet, use a 2-ounce, trigger-release, ice-cream scoop to deposit the batter into the prepared pans so they're three-quarters full.

9. Follow the approximate bake times listed below.

ITEM	SEA LEVEL	HIGH ALTITUDE
12-cup Bundt	45 minutes	60 minutes
Crunchy Feet	14 minutes	25 minutes

10. Once the top of the cake doesn't jiggle in the center, test for doneness by inserting a bamboo skewer in the center of the cake. When the skewer shows just a touch of crumbs the cake is done. The sheen on top may look liquid, but this is normal and comes from the fat in the heavy cream. Remove the pan from the oven and place on a heat-resistant surface or wire rack.

11. For Crunchy Feet, carefully invert the brioche pans to release the cakes 3 to 4 minutes after removing them from the oven—well before they cool completely. You may have to tap each pan firmly—or even slam it—against the sheet pan to release the cake. Place on a heat-resistant surface or wire rack to cool. Immediately soak the pans to make cleaning easier.

12. For the Bundt cake, once the cake has cooled for 5 to 10 minutes, remove the cake by inverting the pan onto a flat surface. Allow it to cool to room temperature, about 30 minutes, before glazing.

SERVING AND STORING

I prefer to eat this cake right away, even when it's hot. It reminds me more of coffee that way. Pour on ample amounts of Glazing Chocolate (page 174) to create a cascade down the sides.

Store under a cake dome at room temperature, or wrapped in plastic in the fridge for up to 1 week. If glazed, store under a cake dome for up to 3 days, or in the fridge for up to 1 week. To store unglazed cake longer, label, date, and store the plastic-wrapped cake in the freezer for up to 1 month.

Clove-Anise Spice Pound Cake

My original aim in making this cake might seem strange—I wanted to blend dry mustard with cloves to create a scent that would register strongly on the olfactory bulb, the home base in the brain for our sense of smell. I like strong, assertive flavors in everything I eat, so I think a cake like this one can be provocative.

This pound cake takes direction from five-spice powder, which contains cloves, cassia (similar to cinnamon), fagara (like pepper), fennel, and star anise. I love blending anise and clove together—I just enjoy smelling the spices before I mix them in.

EQUIPMENT: electric coffee grinder or mortar and pestle, mixing bowls, standing mixer, one 12-cup Bundt pan or small brioche pans

YIELD: one 12-cup Bundt cake or 32 Crunchy Feet

INGREDIENTS

Dry

unbleached all-purpose flour, 13½ ounces (2½ cups + 3 tablespoons), *or 14½ ounces (2¾ cups + 2 tablespoons) at high altitude*

millet, 3 tablespoons

potato starch, 1 tablespoon

vanilla powder, 1½ teaspoons

whole cloves, 1¼ teaspoons

salt, ½ teaspoon

dry yellow mustard, ½ teaspoon

anise seeds, ¾ teaspoon

baking soda, ¼ teaspoon

Liquid

sour cream, 8 ounces (1 cup)

milk, 2 tablespoons, *or 2 tablespoons + 1 teaspoon at high altitude*

rum, 2 tablespoons

vanilla extract, 1½ teaspoons

Creaming

unsalted butter, at room temperature, 8 ounces (2 sticks)

extra-fine granulated sugar, 24 ounces (3 cups), *or 22 ounces (2¾ cups) at high altitude*

eggs (large), 5, *or 6 at high altitude*

yolk (large), 1

Alcohol-free variation: Omit the rum and vanilla extract and substitute 2 tablespoons whole milk. Whisk to combine with the liquid ingredients.

PREPARE AHEAD OF TIME

Pulverize the cloves and anise into a fine powder using an electric spice grinder (I use an electric coffee grinder) or mortar and pestle and set aside.

1. Preheat the oven to 350°F (conventional) or 335°F (convection). Set the rack in the middle of the oven. For Crunchy Feet, set racks in the upper-middle and lower-middle positions.

2. Set out the ingredients and equipment.
- Sift the flour directly into a bowl on a scale for accurate measuring.
- Measure the other dry ingredients into a separate mixing bowl, add the flour, and whisk for 10 seconds to blend. Set aside.
- Measure the liquid ingredients into a separate bowl, whisk to combine, and set aside.
- Measure the butter and sugar into separate bowls and set aside.
- Crack the eggs and yolk into two separate bowls and set aside.

3. In the bowl of a standing mixer fitted with the paddle attachment, cream together the butter and sugar on the lowest speed for 2 to 3 minutes.

4. With the mixer still on the lowest speed, add the eggs one at a time followed by the yolk, fully incorporating after each addition. Stop the mixer and scrape the sides of the bowl.

5. Add the dry ingredient mixture alternately with the liquid mixture in 3 to 5 additions each, beginning and ending with the dry mixture. Move swiftly through this step to avoid overworking the batter. Don't wait for the dry or liquid mixtures to be fully incorporated before adding the next. This step should take a total of about 60 seconds.

6. Stop the mixer and scrape the sides of the bowl all the way down. Don't miss the clumps of ingredients hiding on the bottom of the bowl. Mix on medium speed for 15 to 20 seconds to develop the batter's structure.

7. Prepare the pans. For a Bundt cake, spray the pan well with a nonstick spray. For Crunchy Feet, place the brioche pans on sheet pans (16 per half-sheet pan is a snug fit) and spray them liberally.

8. For a Bundt cake, fill the pan about three-quarters full by depositing the batter with the rubber spatula in small clumps around the prepared pan instead of by pouring it into one spot. Level the batter with the rubber spatula. Bake any leftover batter as Crunchy Feet or cupcakes. For Crunchy Feet, use a 2-ounce, trigger-release, ice-cream scoop to deposit the batter into the prepared pans so they're three-quarters full.

9. Follow the approximate bake times listed below.

ITEM	SEA LEVEL	HIGH ALTITUDE
12-cup Bundt	45 minutes	60 minutes
Crunchy Feet	15 minutes	37 minutes

10. Once the top of the cake doesn't jiggle in the center, test for doneness by inserting a bamboo skewer in the center of the cake. When the skewer shows just a touch of crumbs the cake is done. Remove the pan from the oven and place on a heat-resistant surface or wire rack.

11. For Crunchy Feet, carefully invert the brioche pans to release the cakes 3 to 4 minutes after removing them from the oven—well before they cool completely. You may have to tap each pan firmly— or even slam it—against the sheet pan to release the cake. Place on a heat-resistant surface or wire rack to cool. Immediately soak the pans to make cleaning easier.

12. For the Bundt cake, once the cake has cooled for 5 to 10 minutes, remove the cake by inverting the pan onto a flat surface. Allow it to cool to room temperature, about 30 minutes, before glazing.

SERVING AND STORING

Serve naked or with a dusting of confectioners' sugar. Store under a cake dome at room temperature, or wrapped in plastic in the fridge for up to 1 week. To store longer, label, date, and store the plastic-wrapped cake in the freezer for up to 1 month.

Lemon-Ginger Pound Cake

This is one of the original cakes I created during the hectic days of transitioning from a lawyer into a cake baker. It had a short presence on my menu but I always enjoy it.

Cocoa butter can be a little difficult to find but it's worth the search. Its light, clean, and subtle flavor brings nuances to the cake that people will adore, whether or not they love chocolate. Look for cocoa butter at your local cake decorating or candy making supply store, or at specialty gourmet markets.

EQUIPMENT: rasp or plane zester, mixing bowls, standing mixer, one 12-cup Bundt pan or small brioche pans

YIELD: one 12-cup Bundt cake or 30 Crunchy Feet

INGREDIENTS

Dry

unbleached all-purpose flour, 2 ounces
  (2¼ cups), *or 12½ ounces (2½ cups)*
  at high altitude

potato starch, 1½ tablespoons

baking powder, 1 teaspoon, *or ¾ teaspoon*
  at high altitude

salt, ½ teaspoon

Liquid

light coconut milk, 1 cup, *or 1 cup +*
  1½ tablespoons at high altitude

heavy cream, ¼ cup, *or ¼ cup + 2 teaspoons*
  at high altitude

lemons, 2

orange liqueur, 1 teaspoon

gin, 1 teaspoon

rum, 1 teaspoon

vanilla extract, 2 teaspoons

Creaming

unsalted butter, at room temperature,
  4 ounces (1 stick)

cocoa butter (at room temperature), 4 ounces
  (½ cup)

extra-fine granulated sugar, 14 ounces
  (1¾ cups), *or 13½ ounces (1½ cups +*
  3 tablespoons) at high altitude

confectioners' sugar, 3 ounces (¾ cup),
  or 2¾ ounces (½ cup + 2 tablespoons)
  at high altitude

crystallized ginger, 3 ounces

lemon zest, 3 tablespoons

eggs (large), 4, *or 5 at high altitude*

yolk (large), 1

Alcohol-free variation: Omit the orange liqueur, gin, rum, and vanilla extract. Substitute 2 tablespoons lemon juice. Whisk to combine with the liquid ingredients.

PREPARE AHEAD OF TIME

1. Chop the ginger into ¼-inch pieces.
2. Zest the lemons with a rasp or mince the lemon zest with a chef's knife.
3. Segment the zested lemons (page 206).

1. Preheat the oven to 350°F (conventional) or 335°F (convection). Set the rack in the middle of the oven. For Crunchy Feet, set racks in the upper-middle and lower-middle positions.

2. Set out the ingredients and equipment.

• Sift the flour directly into a bowl on a scale for accurate measuring.

• Measure the other dry ingredients into a separate mixing bowl, add the flour, and whisk for 10 seconds to blend. Set aside.

• Measure the liquid ingredients into a separate bowl, whisk to combine, and set aside.

• Measure the butter, cocoa butter, granulated sugar, confectioners' sugar, ginger, and lemon zest into separate bowls and set aside.

• Crack the eggs and yolk into two separate bowls and set aside.

3. In the bowl of a standing mixer fitted with the paddle attachment, cream together the butter and sugar on the lowest speed for 3 to 4 minutes. The extra time is necessary to slowly blend the various ingredients together.

4. With the mixer still on the lowest speed, add the eggs one at a time followed by the yolk, fully incorporating after each addition. Stop the mixer and scrape the sides of the bowl.

5. Add the dry ingredient mixture alternately with the liquid mixture in 3 to 5 additions each, beginning and ending with the dry mixture. Move swiftly through this step to avoid overworking the batter. Don't wait for the dry or liquid mixtures to be fully incorporated before adding the next. This step should take a total of about 60 seconds.

6. Stop the mixer and scrape the sides of the bowl all the way down. Don't miss the clumps of ingredients hiding on the bottom of the bowl. Mix on medium speed for 15 to 20 seconds to develop the batter's structure.

7. Prepare the pans. For a Bundt cake, spray the pan well with a nonstick spray. For Crunchy Feet, place the brioche pans on sheet pans (16 per half-sheet pan is a snug fit) and spray them liberally.

8. For a Bundt cake, fill the pan about three-quarters full by depositing the batter with the rubber spatula in small clumps around the prepared pan instead of by pouring it into one spot. Level the batter with the rubber spatula. Bake any leftover batter as Crunchy Feet or cupcakes. For Crunchy Feet, use a 2-ounce, trigger-release, ice-cream scoop to deposit the batter into the prepared pans so they're three-quarters full.

9. Follow the approximate bake times listed below.

ITEM	SEA LEVEL	HIGH ALTITUDE
12-cup Bundt	50–55 minutes	65 minutes
Crunchy Feet	15 minutes	34 minutes

10. Once the top of the cake doesn't jiggle in the center, test for doneness by inserting a bamboo skewer in the center of the cake. When the skewer shows just a touch of crumbs the cake is done. The sheen on top may look liquid but this is normal and comes from the fat in the heavy cream. Remove the pan from the oven and place on a heat-resistant surface or wire rack.

11. For Crunchy Feet, carefully invert the brioche pans to release the cakes 3 to 4 minutes after removing them from the oven—well before they cool completely. You may have to tap each pan firmly—or even slam it—against the sheet pan to release the cake. Place on a heat-resistant surface or wire rack to cool. Immediately soak the pans to make cleaning easier.

12. For the Bundt cake, once the cake has cooled for 5 to 10 minutes, remove the cake by inverting the pan onto a flat surface. Allow it to cool to room temperature, about 30 minutes, before glazing.

SERVING AND STORING

Serve naked or with a dusting of confectioners' sugar. To boost flavor and add a special touch, use Lemon Glaze (page 176).

Store under a cake dome at room temperature, or wrapped in plastic in the fridge for up to 1 week. To store longer, label, date, and store the plastic-wrapped cake in the freezer for up to 1 month.

Citron Bundt

> *"There's nothing like a little Citron Bundt to start the day!"*

This is my favorite cake because it's the first recipe I "made up"—the first time I started adding unusual ingredients to a standard pound cake recipe. I was totally nervous and worried it was too weird—who ever heard of putting grapefruit in a cake—but I brought it into work anyway because I knew there was only one way to test it out. Everyone really liked it and they were intrigued at my first foray into baking. Larry Goldberg, one of my colleagues at the time, said one of the nicest and most encouraging things to me that I'll always remember: "There's nothing like a little Citron Bundt to start the day!"

Fresh orange, lemon, and red grapefruit team up with cardamom to create a bouquet of flavors in this tender butter cake. Lemon and orange are the dominant flavors, but the gentle tang of the grapefruit is a pleasant surprise. Cardamom provides a light, lemony background flavor that lingers after the fresh citrus kick fades away.

EQUIPMENT: mortar and pestle, electric coffee grinder, plane zester, 2-quart heavy-bottomed saucepan, standing mixer, mixing bowls, one 12-cup Bundt pan, small brioche pans, or two 9-inch-round pans

YIELD: one 12-cup Bundt cake, 32 Crunchy Feet, or two 9-inch-round cakes

---

INGREDIENTS

Dry

unbleached all-purpose flour, 13½ ounces
  (2½ cups + 3 tablespoons), *or 14 ounces*
  (2¾ cups) at high altitude
potato starch, 1 tablespoon
cardamom pods, 5–7
salt, ¾ teaspoon
baking soda, ¼ teaspoon

Liquid

sour cream, 8 ounces (1 cup)
orange, 1
lemon, 1
red grapefruit, ½
brandy, ¼ cup
vanilla extract, 1 teaspoon
amaretto, ½ teaspoon
dark rum, ½ teaspoon

Creaming

unsalted butter, at room temperature,
  8 ounces (2 sticks)
extra-fine granulated sugar, 21 ounces
  (2½ cups + 2 tablespoons), *or 19¾ ounces*
  (2¼ cups + 3½ tablespoons) at high altitude
citrus zest, 2 tablespoons
eggs (large), 5, *or 6 at high altitude*
yolk (large), 1

Alcohol-free variation: Omit the brandy, vanilla extract, amaretto, and rum. Substitute 2 tablespoons whole milk. Whisk to combine with the liquid ingredients.

PREPARE AHEAD OF TIME

1. Break open the cardamom pods in a mortar and pestle to remove the seeds. Discard the pods and pulverize the seeds into a fine powder using the mortar and pestle or an electric spice or coffee grinder. Set aside.

2. Zest the orange and lemon with a plane zester. Set aside for the creaming stage.

3. Segment the orange, lemon, and grapefruit (page 206).

4. Place the citrus segments in a 2-quart heavy-bottomed saucepan and cover with ½ cup sugar—don't stir. Bring to a gentle simmer over low to medium heat, then promptly remove the pan from the heat. Citrus tends to have a bitter taste if it overcooks. Immediately strain the syrup from the citrus segments and set the segments aside. Reserve the syrup for another use, if desired, or discard it.

1. Preheat the oven to 350°F (conventional) or 335°F (convection). Set the rack in the middle of the oven for cakes. For Crunchy Feet, set racks in the upper-middle and lower-middle positions.

2. Set out the ingredients and equipment.

• Sift the flour directly into a bowl on a scale for accurate measuring.

• Measure the other dry ingredients into a separate mixing bowl, add the flour, and whisk for 10 seconds to blend. Set aside.

• Measure the sour cream, brandy, vanilla extract, amaretto, and rum into a separate bowl. With a rubber spatula, gently fold the cooked citrus segments into the liquid ingredients and set aside.

• Measure the butter and sugar into separate bowls and set aside.

• Crack the eggs and yolk into two separate bowls and set aside.

3. In the bowl of a standing mixer fitted with the paddle attachment, cream together the butter, sugar, and citrus zest on the lowest speed for 2 to 3 minutes. The acids from the citrus zest will

break down the sugar and the creamed mixture will appear a little soggy.

4. With the mixer still on the lowest speed, add the eggs one at a time followed by the yolk, fully incorporating after each addition. Stop the mixer and scrape the sides of the bowl.

5. Add the dry ingredient mixture alternately with the liquid mixture in 3 to 5 additions each, beginning and ending with the dry mixture. Move swiftly through this step to avoid overworking the batter. Don't wait for the dry or liquid mixtures to be fully incorporated before adding the next. This step should take a total of about 60 seconds.

6. Stop the mixer and scrape the sides of the bowl all the way down. Don't miss the clumps of ingredients hiding on the bottom of the bowl. Mix on medium speed for 15 to 20 seconds to develop the batter's structure.

7. Prepare the pans. For a Bundt cake, spray the pan well with a nonstick spray. For Crunchy Feet, place the brioche pans on sheet pans (16 per half-sheet pan is a snug fit) and spray them liberally with a nonstick spray. For 9-inch-round cakes, line the bottom of each pan with parchment but do not spray the sides.

8. For a Bundt cake, fill the pan about three-quarters full by depositing the batter with the rubber spatula in small clumps around the prepared pan instead of by pouring it into one spot. Level the batter with the rubber spatula. Bake any leftover batter as Crunchy Feet or cupcakes. For Crunchy Feet, use a 2-ounce, trigger release, ice-cream scoop to deposit the batter into the prepared pans so they're three-quarters full. For 9-inch-round cakes, deposit the batter into three separate areas of the pan and smooth out with an offset spatula, making sure the pans are two-thirds full.

9. Follow the approximate bake times listed below.

ITEM	SEA LEVEL	HIGH ALTITUDE
12-cup Bundt	50–55 minutes	70 minutes
Crunchy Feet	15 minutes	30 minutes
9-inch rounds	30 minutes	55 minutes

10. Once the top of the cake doesn't jiggle in the center and appears golden blonde across the top, test for doneness by inserting a bamboo skewer in the center of the cake. When the skewer shows just a touch of crumbs or comes out clean, the cake is done. Remove the pan from the oven and place on a heat-resistant surface or wire rack.

11. For Crunchy Feet, carefully invert the brioche pans to release the cakes 3 to 4 minutes after removing them from the oven—well before they cool completely. You may have to tap each pan firmly—or even slam it—against the sheet pan to release the cake. Place on a heat-resistant surface or wire rack to cool. Immediately soak the pans to make cleaning easier.

12. For the Bundt cake, once the cake has cooled for 5 to 10 minutes remove the cake by inverting the pan onto a flat surface. Allow it to cool to room temperature, about 30 minutes, before glazing.

13. For the layer cake, cool to room temperature, 25 to 30 minutes, before removing from the pan. Use a small offset spatula to loosen the cake from the rim of the pan. Carefully invert each pan onto a flat surface to remove the layers. Remove the parchment from the bottom of each cake and wrap the cake tightly in plastic. Assembling a layer cake is easier if the cake is cold, so refrigerate the layers overnight or for up to 5 days before frosting.

SERVING AND STORING

Serve naked or with a dusting of confectioners' sugar. To boost flavor and a give it a beautiful glow, use Apricot Preserve Glaze (page 176).

For extra decadence, I like to fold fresh grapefruit segments into vanilla-flavored Italian Meringue Buttercream (page 151) and serve casually, open-sided (not frosting the sides of cake layers), as in the photo on the facing page. (See page 200 for more information on layering and assembling.)

Store under a cake dome at room temperature, or wrapped in plastic in the fridge for up to 1 week. If frosted, store under a cake dome for up to 3 days, or in the fridge for up to 1 week. To store unfrosted cake longer, label, date, and store the plastic-wrapped cake in the freezer for up to 1 month.

Citron Bundt with vanilla-flavored Italian Meringue Buttercream and sugar-coated grapefruit

Chocolate-Apricot Pound Cake

> *The colors of this cake remind me of a tiger.*

I love the speckles of orange and brown created by combining mini-chunks of apricot and chocolate in this cake. The colors make me think of a tiger, or of my hometown pro football team. You can see that my mind is easily entertained!

Combining dried apricots with bittersweet chocolate against a pleasantly moist yet crunchy butter cake is sinfully satisfying for anyone close enough to catch a whiff of this cake fresh out of the oven. Not too sweet, this batter is quick to mix and a perfect treat for starting or ending any day.

It's understandable if you don't want to use sulphured apricots, but I find the color and texture of unsulphured apricots are not as pleasant in baked goods.

EQUIPMENT: food processor, mixing bowls, standing mixer, one 12-cup Bundt pan or small brioche pans

YIELD: one 12-cup Bundt cake or 24 Crunchy Feet

INGREDIENTS

Dry

unbleached all-purpose flour, 12 ounces (2¼ cups + 2 tablespoons), *or 12½ ounces (2½ cups) at high altitude*

potato starch, 1 tablespoon

baking soda, ¼ teaspoon

salt, ¼ teaspoon

dried apricots, 6 ounces (¾ cup)

extra-fine granulated sugar, 2 tablespoons

cornstarch, 2 teaspoons

60% bittersweet chocolate pistoles, 4 ounces (½ cup)

Liquid

sour cream, 4 ounces (½ cup)

half-and-half, 1 tablespoon

amaretto, ¼ cup

vanilla extract, ½ teaspoon

Creaming

unsalted butter, at room temperature, 5 ounces (1 stick + 2 tablespoons)

extra-fine granulated sugar, 18 ounces (2¼ cups), *or 16 ounces (2 cups) at high altitude*

eggs (large), 4, *or 5 at high altitude*

Chocolate-Apricot Crunchy Feet

Alcohol-free variation: Omit the amaretto and vanilla. Add the seeds of 1 vanilla pod to butter and 1 tablespoon alcohol-free almond extract.

PREPARE AHEAD OF TIME

Pulse the apricots, sugar, and cornstarch in a food processor to chop the fruit into ½-inch pieces. Add the chocolate and continue to pulse 2 to 3 times for three seconds each or until the chocolate is broken into small ½-inch pieces. Set aside to combine with the other dry ingredients.

1. Preheat the oven to 350°F (conventional) or 335°F (convection). Set the rack in the middle of the oven. For Crunchy Feet, set racks in the upper-middle and lower-middle positions.

2. Set out the ingredients and equipment.

• Sift the flour directly into a bowl on a scale for accurate measuring.

• Measure the other dry ingredients into a separate mixing bowl, add the flour, and whisk for 10 seconds to blend. Set aside.

• Measure the liquid ingredients into a separate bowl, whisk to combine, and set aside.

• Measure the butter and sugar into separate bowls and set aside.

• Crack the eggs into a small bowl and set aside.

3. In the bowl of a standing mixer fitted with the paddle attachment, cream together the butter and sugar on the lowest speed for 3 to 4 minutes. Note that this combination won't become very aerated due to lower butter and sugar ratio. The extra fat and sugar in the chocolate means we need to use less during the creaming process.

4. With the mixer still on the lowest speed, add the eggs one at a time, fully incorporating after each addition. Stop the mixer and scrape the sides of the bowl.

5. Add the dry ingredient mixture alternately with the liquid mixture in 3 to 5 additions each, beginning and ending with the dry mixture. Move swiftly through this step to avoid overworking the batter. Don't wait for the dry or liquid mixtures to be fully incorporated before adding the next. This step should take a total of about 60 seconds.

6. Stop the mixer and scrape the sides of the bowl all the way down. Don't miss the clumps of ingredients hiding on the bottom of the bowl. Mix on medium speed for 25 to 30 seconds to develop the batter's structure.

7. Prepare the pans. For a Bundt cake, spray the pan well with a nonstick spray. For Crunchy Feet, place the brioche pans on sheet pans (16 per half-sheet pan is a snug fit) and spray them liberally.

8. For a Bundt cake, fill the pan about three-quarters full by depositing the batter with the rubber spatula in small clumps around the prepared pan instead of by pouring it into one spot. Level the batter with the rubber spatula. Bake any leftover batter as Crunchy Feet or cupcakes. For Crunchy Feet, use a 2-ounce, trigger-release, ice-cream scoop to deposit the batter into the prepared pans so they're three-quarters full.

9. Follow the approximate bake times listed below.

ITEM	SEA LEVEL	HIGH ALTITUDE
12-cup Bundt	45–50 minutes	75 minutes
Crunchy Feet	15 minutes	25 minutes

10. Once the edges of the cake are browning and the surface appears dry, test for doneness by inserting a bamboo skewer in the center of the cake. When the skewer shows just a touch of crumbs except for the smears of melted chocolate, the cake is done. Remove the pan from the oven and place on a heat-resistant surface or wire rack.

11. For Crunchy Feet, carefully invert the brioche pans to release the cakes 3 to 4 minutes after removing them from the oven—well before they cool completely. You may have to tap each pan firmly— or even slam it—against the sheet pan to release the cake. Place on a heat-resistant surface or wire rack to cool. Immediately soak the pans to make cleaning easier.

12. For the Bundt cake, once the cake has cooled for 5 to 10 minutes, remove the cake by inverting the pan onto a flat surface. Allow it to cool to room temperature, about 30 minutes, before glazing.

SERVING AND STORING

I like to top the Bundt cake with the Apricot Preserve Glaze (page 176). The simpler alternative—and my preference—is to bake Crunchy Feet and serve them naked just minutes after they're out of the oven.

Store under a cake dome at room temperature, or wrapped in plastic in the fridge for up to 1 week. To store longer, label, date, and store the plastic-wrapped cake in the freezer for up to 1 month.

Pistoles

The chocolate that I prefer for most recipes for this book is bittersweet chocolate pistoles. I like their flavor, size, and convenience. They melt evenly, taste sensational, and offer a rich brown color for any application. Pistoles are available at specialty gourmet shops and online (see Resources, page 218).

In general, pistoles are easy to work with because they're easy to measure and come in varying percentages of chocolate mass. Giant blocks of chocolate are good to have on hand when irregular shapes are required, but life is a lot easier with the pistole. Please note that chocolate chips aren't quite the same—most are semisweet or milk chocolate and won't melt without some graininess.

Chiapas Pound Cake

> *This cake is inspired by the impressive list of indigenous foods from Chiapas, a state in southeast Mexico.*

Vanilla, polenta, cocoa nibs, honey, cinnamon, cayenne, almonds, and more combine in a dizzying mélange for this recipe. The ancient Olmecs discovered cocoa beans and shared their knowledge with the Mayans, who created a ritual out of making frothy cocoa drinks. It was the Aztecs who added vanilla, honey, and chile pepper for flavor.

EQUIPMENT: food processor, mixing bowls, standing mixer, one 12-cup Bundt pan or small brioche pans

YIELD: one 12-cup Bundt cake or 28 Crunchy Feet

INGREDIENTS

Dry

unbleached all-purpose flour, 12 ounces
    (2¼ cups + 2 tablespoons), *or* 13 ounces
    (2½ cups + 1½ tablespoons)
    at high altitude
cocoa nibs, ¼ cup (1½ ounces)
polenta or cornmeal, ¼ cup (1 ounce)
almond powder (page 63), ¼ cup (1 ounce)
turbinado sugar, 2 tablespoons
potato starch, 1 tablespoon
vanilla powder, 1 tablespoon
baking soda, ¼ teaspoon
salt, ¼ teaspoon
ground cinnamon, ¼ teaspoon
ground cayenne pepper, ⅛ teaspoon

Liquid

crystallized or raw honey, 2 ounces (¼ cup)
half-and-half, ¾ cup, *or* ¾ cup +
    2 tablespoons at high altitude
amaretto, 1 tablespoon
vanilla extract, 2 teaspoons

Creaming

unsalted butter, at room temperature,
    6 ounces (1½ sticks)
extra-fine granulated sugar, 18 ounces
    (2¼ cups), *or 16 ounces (2 cups)*
    at high altitude
eggs (large), 3, *or 4 at high altitude*
yolks (large), 2

Alcohol-free variation: Omit the amaretto and vanilla extract. Substitute 2 tablespoons milk and the seeds scraped from one vanilla bean. Whisk to combine with the liquid ingredients.

PREPARE AHEAD OF TIME

Make the almond powder (page 63). Measure ¼ cup and reserve the remainder for another use.

1. Preheat the oven to 350°F (conventional) or 335°F (convection). Set the rack in the middle of the oven. For Crunchy Feet, set racks in the upper-middle and lower-middle positions.

2. Set out the ingredients and equipment.

• Sift the flour directly into a bowl on a scale for accurate measuring.

• Measure the other dry ingredients into a separate mixing bowl, add the flour, and whisk for 10 seconds to blend. Set aside.

• Measure half-and-half, amaretto, and vanilla extract into a separate bowl, whisk to combine, and set aside. Whisking the honey into the liquids is not necessary.

• Measure the butter and sugar into separate bowls and set aside.

• Crack the eggs and yolks into two separate bowls and set aside.

3. In the bowl of a standing mixer fitted with the paddle attachment, cream together the butter and sugar on the lowest speed for 2 to 3 minutes.

4. With the mixer still on the lowest speed, add the eggs one at a time followed by the yolks, fully incorporating after each addition. Stop the mixture and scrape the sides of the bowl.

5. Add the dry ingredient mixture alternately with the liquid mixture in 3 to 5 additions each, beginning and ending with the dry mixture. The honey may be stubborn and clump in the bowl, so use a rubber spatula to scrape it into the batter as necessary. Move swiftly through this step to avoid overworking the batter. Don't wait for the dry or liquid mixtures to be fully incorporated before adding the next. This step should take a total of about 60 seconds.

6. Stop the mixer and scrape the sides of the bowl all the way down. Don't miss the clumps of ingredients hiding on the bottom of the bowl. Mix on medium speed for 15 to 20 seconds to develop the batter's structure.

7. Prepare the pans. For a Bundt cake, spray the pan well with a nonstick spray. For Crunchy Feet, place the brioche pans on sheet pans (16 per half-sheet pan is a snug fit) and spray them liberally with a nonstick spray.

8. For a Bundt cake, fill the pan about three-quarters full by depositing the batter with the rubber spatula in small clumps around the prepared pan instead of by pouring it into one spot. Level the batter with the rubber spatula. For Crunchy Feet, use a 2-ounce, trigger-release, ice-cream scoop to deposit the batter into the prepared pans so they're three-quarters full.

9. Follow the approximate bake times listed below.

ITEM	SEA LEVEL	HIGH ALTITUDE
12-cup Bundt	50 minutes	60 minutes
Crunchy Feet	15 minutes	30 minutes

10. Once the top of the cake doesn't jiggle, test for doneness by inserting a bamboo skewer in the center of the cake. When the skewer shows just a touch of crumbs or comes out clean, the cake is done. Due to the honey, these cakes will look golden brown across the top and a little darker at the edges. Remove the pan from the oven and place on a heat-resistant surface or wire rack.

11. For Crunchy Feet, carefully invert the brioche pans to release the cakes 3 to 4 minutes after removing them from the oven—well before they cool completely. You may have to tap each pan firmly—or even slam it—against the sheet pan to release the cake. Place on a heat-resistant surface or wire rack to cool. Immediately soak the pans to make cleaning easier.

12. For the Bundt cake, once the cake has cooled for 5 to 10 minutes remove the cake by inverting the pan onto a flat surface. Allow it to cool to room temperature, about 30 minutes, before glazing.

SERVING AND STORING

Serve naked or with a dusting of confectioners' sugar. To boost flavor and add a special touch, use Apricot Preserve Glaze (page 176).

Store under a cake dome at room temperature, or wrapped in plastic in the fridge for up to 1 week. To store longer, label, date, and freeze the plastic-wrapped cake for up to 1 month.

Nut
Powders

This is my preferred method of incorporating nut flavors into a cake or meringues. Processing nuts with confectioners' sugar is better than using flour, which is too heavy for protein-rich nuts; it's also much tastier. This basic preparation is suitable for almonds, pecans, and walnuts. Hazelnuts and peanuts may require more time in the oven.

EQUIPMENT: food processor

YIELD: 2 cups

Ingredients

any hard unsalted nut, 2 ounces (1 cup)
confectioners' sugar, 2 ounces (½ cup)

1. Preheat the oven to 350°F (conventional) or 335°F (convection). Set the rack in the middle of the oven.

2. Place the nuts on a sheet pan lined with parchment and bake for 5 to 7 minutes, or until the nuts are golden brown. Remove the pan from the oven and allow the nuts to cool completely, about 10 to 15 minutes.

3. In the bowl of a food processor, fitted with the steel blade, combine the cooled, toasted nuts with the confectioners' sugar and process to a fine powder, about 30 seconds. Process for longer if you need to or in batches if the work bowl is small.

4. Label, date, and refrigerate in an airtight container until you are ready to use, or for up to 2 weeks.

Mojito Pound Cake with rum-flavored Italian Meringue Buttercream, turbinado sugar, and fresh mint

Mojito Cake

> Whether it's served as a beverage or a cake, the Mojito is always enjoyable.

Modeled after the fabulously thirst-quenching Cuban cocktail, the Mojito Crunchy Feet were an instant hit when introduced at CakeLove. Oddly enough it became a sought-after flavor for wedding cakes, so I panned the batter as a layer cake and paired it with rum-flavored Italian Meringue Buttercream (page 151). I had no idea the result would taste so refreshing. I also like this cake for its speckled appearance and unusual list of ingredients, including cloves, which are barely noticeable but necessary for balance.

For best results use only fresh mint with this spirited cake. Previously dried mint doesn't provide enough flavor. Fresh mint is usually available at grocery stores in the produce section with other fresh herbs. Watch out—drying mint in the oven produces a powerful aroma throughout the house that'll clear the sinuses, so I hope you like mint!

EQUIPMENT: electric coffee grinder, rasp or plane zester, mixing bowls, standing mixer, one 12-cup Bundt pan, small brioche pans, or two 9-inch round pans

YIELD: one 12-cup Bundt cake, 26 Crunchy Feet, or two 9-inch round cakes

INGREDIENTS

Dry

unbleached all-purpose flour, 12 ounces (2¼ cups + 2 tablespoons), or 12½ ounces (2½ cups) at high altitude

potato starch, ¼ cup

salt, 1 teaspoon

vanilla powder, ¼ teaspoon

baking soda, ¼ teaspoon

whole cloves, 3

oven-dried mint (instructions follow), ⅓ cup

Liquid

sour cream, ⅔ cup

half-and-half, ¼ cup, or 6 tablespoons at high altitude

dark rum, 3 tablespoons

vanilla extract, 2 teaspoons

molasses, 1 teaspoon

limoncello, 1 teaspoon

lime, 1

Creaming

unsalted butter, at room temperature, 8 ounces (2 sticks)

extra-fine granulated sugar, 10 ounces (2¼ cups), or 16½ ounces (2 cups + 1 tablespoon) at high altitude

minced lime zest, 2 teaspoons

eggs (large), 4, or 5 at high altitude

yolks (large), 2

Alcohol-free variation: This one is difficult to re-create without the rum, but not impossible. Omit the rum, vanilla extract, and limoncello. Add the seeds from 1 vanilla bean, 2 tablespoons fresh lemon juice, and 1 additional teaspoon of molasses. Whisk to combine with the liquid ingredients.

PREPARE AHEAD OF TIME

1. Pulverize the cloves into a fine powder using an electric coffee grinder or mortar and pestle. Set aside.

2. Enclose the mint in an aluminum foil pouch perforated on both sides (use a fork to poke the holes). Dry the fresh mint in a 350°F preheated oven. It will take about 10 to 15 minutes—check often. Remove the pouch from the oven to cool. Run your fingers along the cooled stems to remove the dried leaves. Crush the leaves between your fingers and set aside.

3. Zest the lime with a rasp or mince the zest with a chef's knife.

4. Segment the zested lime (page 206).

1. Preheat the oven to 350°F (conventional) or 335°F (convection). Set the rack in the middle of the oven for Bundt or round layer cakes. For Crunchy Feet, set racks in the upper-middle and lower-middle positions.

2. Set out the ingredients and equipment.

• Sift the flour directly into a bowl on a scale for accurate measuring.

• Measure the other dry ingredients into a separate mixing bowl, add the flour, and whisk for 10 seconds to blend. Set aside.

• Measure the liquid ingredients into a separate bowl, whisk to combine, and set aside. Don't try to break up the lime segments—the mixer will take care of that.

• Measure the butter and sugar into separate bowls and set aside.

• Crack the eggs and yolks into two separate bowls and set aside.

3. In the bowl of a standing mixer fitted with the paddle attachment, cream together the butter, sugar, and lime zest on the lowest speed for 4 to 5 minutes.

4. With the mixer still on the lowest speed, add the eggs one at a time followed by the yolks, fully incorporating after each addition.

5. Add the dry ingredient mixture alternately with the liquid mixture in 3 to 5 additions each, beginning and ending with the dry mixture. Move swiftly through this step to avoid overworking the batter. Don't wait for the dry or liquid mixtures to be fully incorporated before adding the next. This step should take a total of about 60 seconds.

6. Stop the mixer and scrape the sides of the bowl all the way down. Raise the paddle from the batter, free any lime segments stuck to it, and add them back into the batter. Don't miss the clumps of ingredients hiding on the bottom of the bowl. Mix on medium speed for 15 to 20 seconds to develop the batter's structure.

7. Prepare the pans. For a Bundt cake, spray the pan well with a nonstick spray. For Crunchy Feet, place the brioche pans on sheet pans (16 per half-sheet pan is a snug fit) and spray them liberally with a nonstick spray. For 9-inch-round cakes, line the bottom of each pan with parchment but do not spray the sides.

8. For a Bundt cake, fill the pan about three-quarters full by depositing the batter with the rubber spatula in small clumps around the prepared pan instead of by pouring it into one spot. Level the batter with the rubber spatula. Bake any leftover batter as Crunchy Feet or cupcakes. For Crunchy Feet, use a 2-ounce, trigger-release, ice-cream scoop to deposit the batter into the prepared pans so they're three-quarters full. For 9-inch-round cakes, deposit the batter into three separate areas of the pan and smooth out with an offset spatula, making sure the pans are two-thirds full.

9. Follow the approximate bake times listed below.

ITEM	SEA LEVEL	HIGH ALTITUDE
12-cup Bundt	45–50 minutes	50 minutes
Crunchy Feet	15 minutes	30 minutes
9-inch rounds	30 minutes	47–52 minutes

10. Once the top of the cake doesn't jiggle in the center and the surface looks blonde with browned edges, test for doneness by inserting a bamboo skewer in the center of the cake. When the skewer shows just a touch of crumbs or comes out clean, the cake is done. Remove the pan from the oven and place on a heat-resistant surface or wire rack.

11. For the Bundt cake, once the cake has cooled for 5 to 10 minutes, remove the cake by inverting the pan onto a flat surface. Allow it to cool to room temperature, about 30 minutes, before glazing.

12. For Crunchy Feet, carefully invert the brioche pans to release the cakes 3 to 4 minutes after removing them from the oven—well before they cool completely. You may have to tap each pan firmly—or even slam it—against the sheet pan to release the cake. Place on a heat-resistant surface or wire rack to cool. Immediately soak the pans to make cleaning easier.

13. For the layer cake, cool to room temperature, 25 to 30 minutes, before removing from the pan. Use a small offset spatula to loosen the cake from the rim of the pan. Carefully invert each pan onto a flat surface to remove the layers. Remove the parchment from the bottom of each cake and wrap the cake tightly in plastic. Assembling a layer cake is easier if the cake is cold, so refrigerate the layers overnight or for up to 5 days before frosting.

SERVING AND STORING

For the Bundt, I suggest using the Spiced Glaze (page 177). The Crunchy Feet are great naked or with a dusting of confectioners' sugar. The layer cake is best frosted with the rum flavored Italian Meringue Buttercream (page 151). (See page 200 for more information on layering and assembling.)

Store under a cake dome at room temperature, or wrapped in plastic in the fridge for up to 1 week. If frosted, store under a cake dome for up to 3 days, or in the fridge for up to 1 week. To store unfrosted cake longer, label, date, and store the plastic-wrapped cake in the freezer for up to 1 month.

Peanut-Raisin Pound Cake

There is a "best bite" in every meal and for me one of the best bites of all is the middle of a peanut butter and jelly sandwich. You know the bite, where the jelly is threatening to drip off the edge and globs of peanut butter are stuck to the corners of your mouth. Well, I was inspired in a moment of hunger-induced daydreaming when I envisioned that bite, and instantly craved it in cake.

Re-creating this glorious moment in cake form is a challenge. For starters, don't break up the peanuts. Peanuts are very fatty and when crushed too small their oil leaches out during baking and can result in a chewy cake that tastes rancid after only a few days. Leaving the peanuts whole makes a big difference.

EQUIPMENT: mixing bowls, standing mixer, one 12-cup Bundt pan or small brioche pans

YIELD: one 12-cup Bundt cake or 28 Crunchy Feet

INGREDIENTS

Dry

unbleached all-purpose flour, 13 ounces (2½ cups+ 3 tablespoons), *or 13½ ounces (2½ cups + 3 tablespoons) at high altitude*

unsalted peanuts, 4 ounces (¾ cup)

raisins, 5 ounces (1 cup)

potato starch, 1 tablespoon

baking soda, ¼ teaspoon

salt, ¼ teaspoon

Liquid

turbinado sugar, 2 tablespoons

half-and-half, ½ cup, *or ½ cup + 1 tablespoon + 2 teaspoons at high altitude*

sour cream, ¼ cup

heavy cream, 2 tablespoons, *or 2 tablespoons + 1 teaspoon at high altitude*

vanilla extract, 2 teaspoons

Creaming

unsalted butter, at room temperature, 5 ounces (1 stick + 2 tablespoons)

extra-fine granulated sugar, 12 ounces (1½ cups), *or 11½ ounces (1¼ cups + 3 tablespoons) at high altitude*

turbinado sugar, 2 tablespoons

eggs (large), 4, *or 5 at high altitude*

PREPARE AHEAD OF TIME

Place the peanuts on a parchment–lined sheet pan and roast at 350°F for 5 to 7 minutes, or until they're golden brown. Set aside to cool to room temperature.

1. Preheat the oven to 350°F (conventional) or 335°F (convection). Set the rack in the middle of the oven. For Crunchy Feet, set racks in the upper-middle and lower-middle positions.

2. Set out the ingredients and equipment.

• Sift the flour directly into a bowl on a scale for accurate measuring.

• Measure the other dry ingredients into a separate mixing bowl, add the flour, and whisk for 10 seconds to blend. Set aside.

• Measure the liquid ingredients into the bowl of a food processor. Process for 2 minutes, or until the mixture is completely smooth.

• Measure the butter and sugars into separate bowls and set aside.

• Crack the eggs into a bowl and set aside.

3. In the bowl of a standing mixer fitted with the paddle attachment, cream together the butter and sugars on the lowest speed for 4 to 5 minutes.

4. With the mixer still on the lowest speed, add the eggs one at a time, fully incorporating after each addition. Stop the mixer and scrape the sides of the bowl.

5. Add the dry ingredient mixture alternately with the liquid mixture in 3 to 5 additions each, beginning and ending with the dry mixture. Move swiftly through this step to avoid overworking the batter. Don't wait for the dry or liquid mixtures to be fully incorporated before adding the next. This step should take a total of about 60 seconds.

6. Stop the mixer and scrape the sides of the bowl all the way down. Don't miss the clumps of ingredients hiding on the bottom of the bowl. Mix on medium speed for 15 to 20 seconds to develop the batter's structure.

7. Prepare the pans. For a Bundt cake, spray the pan well with a nonstick spray. For Crunchy Feet, place the brioche pans on sheet pans (16 per half-sheet pan is a snug fit) and spray them liberally.

8. For a Bundt cake, fill the pan about three-quarters full by depositing the batter with the rubber spatula in small clumps around the prepared pan instead of by pouring it into one spot. Level the batter with the rubber spatula. Bake any leftover batter as Crunchy Feet or cupcakes. For Crunchy Feet, use a 2-ounce, trigger-release, ice-cream scoop to deposit the batter into the prepared pans so they're three-quarters full.

9. Follow the approximate bake times listed below.

ITEM	SEA LEVEL	HIGH ALTITUDE
12-cup Bundt	45 minutes	66 minutes
Crunchy Feet	15 minutes	25 minutes

10. Once the top of the cake doesn't jiggle in the center, test for doneness by inserting a bamboo skewer in the center of the cake. When the skewer shows just a touch of crumbs or comes out clean, the cake is done. Remove the pan from the oven and place on a heat-resistant surface or wire rack.

11. For Crunchy Feet, carefully invert the brioche pans to release the cakes 3 to 4 minutes after removing them from the oven—well before they cool completely. You may have to tap each pan firmly—or even slam it—against the sheet pan to release the cake. Place on a heat-resistant surface or wire rack to cool. Immediately soak the pans to make cleaning easier.

12. For the Bundt cake, once the cake has cooled for 5 to 10 minutes, remove the cake by inverting the pan onto a flat surface. Allow it to cool to room temperature, about 30 minutes, before glazing.

SERVING AND STORING

Serve at room temperature either naked or with a dusting of confectioners' sugar.

Store under a cake dome at room temperature, or wrapped in plastic in the fridge for up to 1 week. To store longer, label, date, and store the plastic-wrapped cake in the freezer for up to 2 weeks.

Pumpkin-Clove Pound Cake with vanilla-mace Italian Meringue Buttercream and ground cinnamon

Pumpkin-Clove Pound Cake

> *Pumpkin is great for baking anytime of the year.*

I originally baked this cake for my friend Chris who wanted something special for Thanksgiving. We went to law school together and both had a blast in the law-school follies, where we mocked our law-student lifestyles—it wasn't all studying, but there sure was a lot of it. He inspired me by taking a sabbatical from practicing law to develop his passion for theater and acting. He's the first person I knew who proved that leaving the law was possible.

The one thing I wanted out of a pumpkin cake was to avoid the oily mess that is so common with pumpkin breads and muffins. Using butter instead of oil and cutting back on the liquid ingredients to accommodate the heavy, super-moist canned pumpkin did the trick. Still, this is a very wet, heavy batter so aerating the cake well during creaming is extremely important. This recipe also produces a lot of batter so you may need to scrape down the sides of the bowl more frequently than in other recipes to be sure the batter is well mixed. The testing skewer will remain very wet up to the moment the cake is ready to be removed from the oven, so watch it carefully.

This cake is not only a seasonal favorite at CakeLove, but also one of the most popular year-round.

EQUIPMENT: mixing bowls, standing mixer, one 12-cup Bundt pan, small brioche pans, or two 9-inch round pans

YIELD: one 12-cup Bundt cake, 32 Crunchy Feet, or two 9-inch round cakes

INGREDIENTS

Dry

unbleached all-purpose flour, 14 ounces
(2¾ cups), *or 14½ ounces (2¾ cups +*
1½ tablespoons) at high altitude

turbinado sugar, ¼ cup, *or 3 tablespoons*
at high altitude

baking powder, 1 tablespoon, *or 2 teaspoons*
at high altitude

vanilla powder, 1½ teaspoons

salt, ½ teaspoon

ground cloves, 1¼ teaspoons

ground allspice, ⅛ teaspoon

Liquid

canned pumpkin, 15 ounces

heavy cream, 5 tablespoons, *or 6 tablespoons*
at high altitude

dark rum, 1 tablespoon

raw honey, 1 tablespoon

vanilla extract, 1 tablespoon

Creaming

unsalted butter, at room temperature,
6 ounces (1½ sticks), *or 8 ounces*
(2 sticks) at high altitude

extra-fine granulated sugar, 21 ounces
(2½ cups + 2 tablespoons), *or 19¾ ounces*
(2¼ cups + 3 tablespoons + 1 teaspoon)
at high altitude

eggs (large), 2, *or 3 at high altitude*

yolks (large), 4

Alcohol-free variation: Omit the rum and vanilla extract.

1. Preheat the oven to 350°F (conventional) or 335°F (convection). Set the rack in the middle of the oven. For Crunchy Feet, set racks in the upper-middle and lower-middle positions.

2. Set out the ingredients and equipment.

• Sift the flour directly into a bowl on a scale for accurate measuring.

• Measure the other dry ingredients into a separate mixing bowl, add the flour, and whisk for 10 seconds to blend. Set aside.

• Measure the liquid ingredients into a separate bowl, whisk to combine, and set aside.

• Measure the butter and sugar into separate bowls and set aside.

• Crack the eggs and yolks into two separate bowls and set aside.

3. In the bowl of a standing mixer fitted with the paddle attachment, cream together the butter and sugar on the lowest speed for 3 minutes. This is a very dense cake so aerating well is important.

4. With the mixer still on the lowest speed, add the eggs one at a time followed by the yolks, fully incorporating after each addition. Stop the mixture and scrape the sides of the bowl.

5. Add the dry ingredient mixture alternately with the liquid mixture in 3 to 5 additions each, beginning and ending with the dry mixture. Move swiftly through this step to avoid overworking the batter. Don't wait for the dry or liquid mixtures to be fully incorporated before adding the next. This step should take a total of about 60 seconds.

6. Stop the mixer and scrape the sides of the bowl all the way down. Don't miss the clumps of ingredients hiding on the bottom of the bowl. Mix on medium speed for 15 to 20 seconds to develop the batter's structure.

7. Prepare the pans. For a Bundt cake, spray the pan well with a nonstick spray. For Crunchy Feet, place the brioche pans on sheet pans (16 per half-sheet pan is a snug fit) and spray them liberally with a nonstick spray. For 9-inch-round cakes, line the bottom of each pan with parchment but do not spray the sides.

8. For a Bundt cake, fill the pan about three-quarters full by depositing the batter with the rubber spatula in small clumps around the prepared pan instead of by pouring it into one spot. Level the batter with the rubber spatula. Bake any leftover batter as Crunchy Feet or cupcakes. For Crunchy Feet, use a 2-ounce, trigger-release, ice-cream scoop to deposit the batter into the prepared pans so they're three-quarters full. For 9-inch-round cakes, deposit the batter into three separate areas of the pan and smooth out with an offset spatula, making sure the pans are two-thirds full.

9. Follow the approximate bake times listed below.

ITEM	SEA LEVEL	HIGH ALTITUDE
12-cup Bundt	40–55 minutes	65–70 minutes
Crunchy Feet	15 minutes	30 minutes
9-inch rounds	30 minutes	55 minutes

10. Once the top of the cake doesn't jiggle in the center and the color is an even, deep orange, test for doneness by inserting a bamboo skewer in the center of the cake. When the skewer shows just a touch of crumbs or comes out clean, the cake is done. Remove the pan from the oven and place on a heat-resistant surface or wire rack.

11. For the Bundt cake, once the cake has cooled for 5 to 10 minutes, remove it by inverting the pan onto a flat surface. Allow it to cool to room temperature, about 30 minutes, before glazing.

12. For Crunchy Feet, carefully invert the brioche pans to release the cakes 3 to 4 minutes after removing them from the oven—well before they cool completely. You may have to tap each pan firmly—or even slam it—against the sheet pan to release the cake. Place on a heat-resistant surface or wire rack to cool. Immediately soak the pans to make cleaning easier.

13. For the layer cake, cool to room temperature, 25 to 30 minutes, before removing from the pan. Use a small offset spatula to loosen the cake from the rim of the pan. Carefully invert each pan onto a flat surface to remove the layers. Remove the parchment from the bottom of each cake and wrap the cake tightly in plastic. Assembling a layer cake is easier if the cake is cold, so refrigerate the layers overnight or for up to 5 days before frosting.

SERVING AND STORING

Serve at room temperature either naked or with a dusting of confectioners' sugar. The Spiced Glaze (page 176) works very well for a basic but slightly dressed-up presentation.

For maximum decadence, pair the Bundt or layer cake with a vanilla-mace buttercream—add 2 teaspoons ground mace and 2 teaspoons vanilla extract to the Italian Meringue Buttercream (page 151), as on page 70. (See page 200 for more information on layering and assembling.) The eggnog aroma will create instant holiday spirits.

Store under a cake dome at room temperature, or wrapped in plastic in the fridge for up to 1 week. If frosted, store under a cake dome for up to 3 days, or in the fridge for up to 1 week. To store unfrosted cake longer, label, date, and store the plastic-wrapped cake in the freezer for up to 1 month.

Rum Runner

This pound cake is suitable anytime of year, but under the hood of this Bundt is enough rum to keep anyone feeling warm when it's cold outside.

EQUIPMENT: mixing bowls, standing mixer, one 12-cup Bundt pan or small brioche pans

YIELD: one 12-cup Bundt cake or 32 Crunchy Feet

INGREDIENTS

Dry

unbleached all-purpose flour, 14 ounces
(2¾ cups + ½ teaspoon), *or 14½ ounces
(2¾ cups + 1 tablespoon + 1 teaspoon)
at high altitude*

dark muscovado or brown sugar,
¼ cup, packed

potato starch, 2 tablespoons

vanilla powder, 1 teaspoon

salt, ½ teaspoon

ground cinnamon, ½ teaspoon

baking soda, ¼ teaspoon

Liquid

sour cream, 8 ounces (1 cup)

heavy cream, ¾ cup, *or ¾ cup +
2 tablespoons at high altitude*

dark rum, ¼ cup

molasses, 1 teaspoon

vanilla extract, 1 teaspoon

Creaming

unsalted butter, at room temperature,
8 ounces (2 sticks)

extra-fine granulated sugar, 20 ounces
(2½ cups), *or 18¾ ounces (2¼ cups +
1½ tablespoons) at high altitude*

vanilla bean, ½

eggs (large), 4, *or 5 at high altitude*

yolks (large), 2

Rum Soaking Syrup

Sugar Syrup (page 210), ¼ cup

dark rum, ¼ cup

Alcohol-free variation: It's quite a challenge to make rum cake without alcohol. Still, a very good cake can be made if you omit the rum and vanilla extract and substitute 2 tablespoons milk.

1. Preheat the oven to 350°F (conventional) or 335°F (convection). Set the rack in the middle of the oven. For Crunchy Feet, set racks in the upper-middle and lower-middle positions.

2. Set out the ingredients and equipment.

• Sift the flour directly into a bowl on a scale for accurate measuring.

• Measure the other dry ingredients into a separate mixing bowl, break up the dark muscovado or brown sugar, add the flour, and whisk for 10 seconds to blend. Set aside.

• Measure the liquid ingredients into a separate bowl, whisk to combine, and set aside.

• Measure the butter and sugar into separate bowls and set aside.

• Crack the eggs and yolks into two separate bowls and set aside.

3. In the bowl of a standing mixer fitted with the paddle

attachment, cream together the butter and sugar on the lowest speed for 2 to 3 minutes.

4. Meanwhile, slice the vanilla bean lengthwise with a paring knife. From one half of the pod, scrape out the seeds. Add the seeds to the creaming butter and sugar. Reserve the other half of the pod for another use.

5. With the mixer still on the lowest speed, add the eggs one at a time followed by the yolks, fully incorporating after each addition. Stop the mixer and scrape the sides of the bowl.

6. Add the dry ingredient mixture alternately with the liquid mixture in 3 to 5 additions each, beginning and ending with the dry mixture. Move swiftly through this step to avoid overworking the batter. Don't wait for the dry or liquid mixtures to be fully incorporated before adding the next. This step should take a total of about 60 seconds.

7. Stop the mixer and scrape the sides of the bowl all the way down. Don't miss the clumps of ingredients hiding on the bottom of the bowl. Mix on medium speed for 15 to 20 seconds to develop the batter's structure.

8. Prepare the pans. For a Bundt cake, spray the pan well with a nonstick spray. For Crunchy Feet, place the brioche pans on sheet pans (16 per half-sheet pan is a snug fit) and spray them liberally with a nonstick spray.

9. For a Bundt cake, fill the pan about three-quarters full by depositing the batter with the rubber spatula in small clumps around the prepared pan instead of by pouring it into one spot. Level the batter with the rubber spatula. Bake any leftover batter as Crunchy Feet or cupcakes. For Crunchy Feet, use a 2-ounce, trigger-release, ice-cream scoop to deposit the batter into the prepared pans so they're three-quarters full.

10. Follow the approximate bake times listed below.

ITEM	SEA LEVEL	HIGH ALTITUDE
12-cup Bundt	50 minutes	57 minutes
Crunchy Feet	18 minutes	30 minutes

11. Once the top of the cake doesn't jiggle in the center, test for doneness by inserting a bamboo skewer in the center of the cake. When the skewer shows just a touch of crumbs or comes out clean, the cake is done. The sheen on top may look liquid but this is normal and comes from the fat in the heavy cream. Remove the pan from the oven and place on a heat-resistant surface or wire rack.

12. For Crunchy Feet, carefully invert the brioche pans to release the cakes 3 to 4 minutes after removing them from the oven—well before they cool completely. You may have to tap each pan firmly— or even slam it—against the sheet pan to release the cake. Place on a heat-resistant surface or wire rack to cool. Immediately soak the pans to make cleaning easier.

13. For the Bundt cake, once the cake has cooled for 5 to 10 minutes remove it by inverting the pan onto a flat surface. Allow it to cool to room temperature, about 30 minutes, before glazing.

14. Set the cake on a wire rack with wax or parchment paper underneath it to catch any dripping syrup. Combine the Sugar Syrup and rum in a small bowl. Apply the soaking syrup with a pastry brush until all of the syrup is absorbed.

SERVING AND STORING

Serve at room temperature either naked or with a dusting of confectioners' sugar.

For more rum flavor, pair this Bundt with a vanilla-rum buttercream to the Italian Meringue Buttercream (page 151), add 2 to 4 tablespoons dark rum and 2 teaspoons vanilla extract.

Store under a cake dome at room temperature, or wrapped in plastic in the fridge for up to 1 week. If frosted, store under a cake dome for up to 3 days, or in the fridge for up to 1 week. To store unfrosted cake longer, label, date, and store the plastic-wrapped cake in the freezer for up to 1 month.

Stout Pound Cake with Roasted Pecans

The deep, dark color and flavor of stout pairs well with the molasses-like flavor of dark brown sugar and roasted pecans. When I offered samples of this at the bakery, people dived in and gushed about the nuts. The carbonation from the stout gives it a unique spongy texture that is heavenly soft and moist. Enjoy!

EQUIPMENT: 2-quart heavy-bottomed saucepan, mixing bowls, standing mixer, one 12-cup Bundt pan or small brioche pans

YIELD: one 12-cup Bundt cake or 28 Crunchy Feet

INGREDIENTS

Dry

unbleached all-purpose flour, 14 ounces
   (2¾ cups), *or 14½ ounces (2¾ cups +*
   1½ tablespoons) at high altitude

pecans, 3 ounces

cornstarch, 2 teaspoons

ground cloves, 1¼ teaspoons

salt, ½ teaspoon

baking soda, ¼ teaspoon

Liquid

reduced dark stout, 8 ounces (1 cup),
   or 9¼ ounces (1 cup + 2 tablespoons
   + 1 teaspoon) at high altitude

heavy cream, ¼ cup, *or ¼ cup + 2 teaspoons*
   at high altitude

vanilla extract, 1½ teaspoons

Creaming

unsalted butter, at room temperature,
   6 ounces (1½ sticks)

extra-fine granulated sugar, 16 ounces
   (2 cups), *or 15 ounces (1¾ cup +*
   2 tablespoons), at high altitude

dark muscovado or brown sugar, 2 ounces

eggs (large), 3, *or 4 at high altitude*

yolks (large), 2

Whiskey Soaking Syrup

Sugar Syrup (page 210), ¼ cup

Irish whiskey, 2 tablespoons

PREPARE AHEAD OF TIME

1. Bring 12 ounces of stout to a simmer over medium heat in a 2-quart heavy-bottomed saucepan and reduce by one-third, to 8 ounces (9¼ ounces for high altitude). This will take 5 to 10 minutes.

2. Roast the pecans on a sheet pan in a 350°F preheated oven for about 7 minutes, or until you can just begin to smell them. Allow the pecans to cool completely before gently crumbling them with your fingers into blueberry-sized pieces.

1. Preheat the oven to 350°F (conventional) or 335°F (convection). Set the rack in the middle of the oven. For Crunchy Feet, set racks in the upper-middle and lower-middle positions.

2. Set out the ingredients and equipment.

• Sift the flour directly into a bowl on a scale for accurate measuring.

• Measure the other dry ingredients, including the pecans, into a separate mixing bowl, add the flour, and whisk for 10 seconds to blend. Set aside.

• Measure the liquid ingredients into a separate bowl, whisk to combine, and set aside.

• Measure the butter and sugars into separate bowls and set aside.

• Crack the eggs and yolks into two separate bowls and set aside.

3. In the bowl of a standing mixer fitted with the paddle attachment, cream together the butter and sugars on the lowest speed for 2 to 3 minutes.

4. With the mixer still on the lowest speed, add the eggs one at a time followed by the yolks, fully incorporating after each addition.

5. Add the dry ingredient mixture alternately with the liquid mixture in 3 to 5 additions each, beginning and ending with the dry mixture. Move swiftly through this step to avoid overworking the batter. Don't wait for the dry or liquid mixtures to be fully incorporated before adding the next. This step should take a total of about 60 seconds.

6. Stop the mixer and scrape the sides of the bowl all the way down. Don't miss the clumps of ingredients hiding on the bottom of the bowl. Mix on medium speed for 15 to 20 seconds to develop the batter's structure.

7. Prepare the pans. For a Bundt cake, spray the pan well with a nonstick spray. For Crunchy Feet, place the brioche pans on sheet pans (16 per half-sheet pan is a snug fit) and spray them liberally.

8. For a Bundt cake, fill the pan about three-quarters full by depositing the batter with the rubber spatula in small clumps around the prepared pan instead of by pouring it into one spot. Level the batter with the rubber spatula. Bake any leftover batter as Crunchy Feet or cupcakes. For Crunchy Feet, use a 2-ounce, trigger-release, ice-cream scoop to deposit the batter into the prepared pans so they're three-quarters full.

9. Follow the approximate bake times listed below.

ITEM	SEA LEVEL	HIGH ALTITUDE
12-cup Bundt	50–55 minutes	60 minutes
Crunchy Feet	14–15 minutes	27 minutes

10. Once the top of the cake doesn't jiggle in the center and is light brown, test for doneness by inserting a bamboo skewer in the center of the cake. When the skewer shows just a touch of crumbs or comes out clean, the cake is done. The sheen on top may look liquid but this is normal and comes from the fat in the heavy cream. Remove the pan from the oven and place on a heat-resistant surface or wire rack.

11. For Crunchy Feet, carefully invert the brioche pans to release the cakes 3 to 4 minutes after removing them from the oven—well before they cool completely. You may have to tap each pan firmly—or even slam it—against the sheet pan to release the cake. Place on a heat-resistant surface or wire rack to cool. Immediately soak the pans to make cleaning easier.

12. For the Bundt cake, once the cake has cooled for 5 to 10 minutes remove the cake by inverting the pan onto a flat surface. Allow it to cool to room temperature, about 30 minutes, before glazing.

13. Set the cake on a wire rack with wax or parchment paper underneath it to catch any dripping syrup. Combine the Sugar Syrup and Irish whiskey in a small bowl. Apply the soaking syrup with a pastry brush until all of the syrup is absorbed.

SERVING AND STORING

Serve at room temperature either naked or with a dusting of confectioners' sugar.

Store under a cake dome at room temperature, or wrapped in plastic in the fridge for up to 1 week. To store longer, label, date, and store the plastic-wrapped cake in the freezer for up to 1 month.

Extra-fine + turbinado sugar = use less sugar

Sometimes I combine extra-fine granulated sugar with turbinado sugar—extra-large chunky sugar crystals—in the creaming stage. In small amounts it acts as a catalyst for creaming butter and sugar: the bulky turbinado rapidly penetrates the butter and accelerates each step of the aeration. The advantage of using turbinado is that it allows me to cut back on the total amount of sugar without losing too much air. I tend to substitute 1 tablespoon of turbinado for 2 ounces of extra-fine granulated sugar, up to a maximum of 3 tablespoons of turbinado in a recipe.

Triple Lime–Chocolate Crunchy Feet

The salt-and-sugar crust makes these Crunchy Feet taste like margaritas.

I was inspired to bake these Crunchy Feet after overhearing a customer on line at CakeLove say they love the combination of chocolate and lime. After thinking about ways to max out these two distinct flavors I stumbled on the idea of introducing cream cheese during the creaming stage. The cream cheese helps aerate the batter while contributing only a neutral, mildly tangy flavor, clearing the way for chocolate and lime to take center stage. Using all butter would taste great but could obstruct the gentle interplay of chocolate and lime that happens in each bite.

EQUIPMENT: rasp or plane zester, mixing bowls, standing mixer, small brioche pans

YIELD: 26 Crunchy Feet

INGREDIENTS

Dry

unbleached all-purpose flour, 10 ounces (2 cups), or *10½ ounces (2 cups + 1 tablespoon + 2 teaspoons) at high altitude*

potato starch, 3 tablespoons

kosher salt, ½ teaspoon

baking soda, ¼ teaspoon

bittersweet chocolate pistoles, 4 ounces (½ cup)

Liquid

limes, 2

sour cream, 4 ounces (½ cup)

whole milk, ¼ cup, or *¼ cup + 2 teaspoons at high altitude*

heavy cream, 2 tablespoons, or *2 tablespoons + 1 teaspoon at high altitude*

amaretto, 2 teaspoons

vanilla extract, 1 teaspoon

lime oil, ¼ teaspoon

Creaming

unsalted butter, at room temperature, 4 ounces (1 stick)

cream cheese, 2 ounces

extra-fine granulated sugar, 16 ounces (2 cups), or *15 ounces at high altitude*

turbinado sugar, 2 tablespoons

lime zest, 2 tablespoons

eggs (large), 3, or *4 at high altitude*

yolks (large), 3

Crust

turbinado sugar, 2 tablespoons

kosher salt, 1 teaspoon

Alcohol-free variation: Use alcohol-free almond extract instead of amaretto and ½ vanilla bean instead of the vanilla extract.

PREPARE AHEAD OF TIME

1. Zest the lime with a rasp and mince the lime zest with a chef's knife. Set aside.
2. Segment the zested lime (page 206).
3. If you're not using pistoles, gently break the chocolate into ¼-inch pieces. Set aside.
4. For the crust, stir together the turbinado sugar and kosher salt in a small bowl and set aside.

Preheat the oven to 350°F (conventional) or 335°F (convection) and set racks in the upper-middle and lower-middle positions.

Set out the ingredients and equipment.

• Sift the flour directly into a bowl on a scale for accurate measuring.
• Measure the other dry ingredients into a separate mixing bowl, add the flour, and whisk for 10 seconds to blend. Set aside.
• Measure the liquid ingredients into a separate bowl, whisk to combine, and set aside. Don't try to break up the lime segments—the mixer will take care of that.
• Measure the butter, cream cheese, and sugars into separate bowls and set aside.
• Crack the eggs and yolks into two separate bowls and set aside.

In a free-standing mixer fitted with the paddle attachment, cream together the butter, cream cheese, sugars, and lime zest on the lowest speed for 3 to 4 minutes.

With the mixer still on the lowest speed, add the eggs one at a time followed by the yolks, fully incorporating after each addition.

Add the dry ingredient mixture alternately with the liquid mixture in 3 to 5 additions each, beginning and ending with the dry mixture. Move swiftly through this step to avoid overworking the batter. Don't wait for the dry or liquid mixtures to be fully incorporated before adding the next. This step should take a total of about 60 seconds.

Stop the mixer and scrape the sides of the bowl all the way down. Don't miss the clumps of ingredients hiding on the bottom of the bowl. Mix on medium speed for 20 to 25 seconds to develop the batter's structure.

Prepare the pans. Place the brioche pans on sheet pans (16 per half-sheet pan is a snug fit) and spray them liberally with a nonstick spray. Sprinkle a pinch (less than ¼ teaspoon) of the sugar-salt mixture into the bottom of each pan.

Use a 2-ounce, trigger-release, ice-cream scoop to deposit the batter into the prepared pans so they're three-quarters full.

Follow the approximate bake times listed below.

ITEM	SEA LEVEL	HIGH ALTITUDE
Crunchy Feet	15 minutes	38 minutes

Once the tops of the cakes don't jiggle in the center, and they look blonde across the center and browned around the edges, test for doneness by inserting a bamboo skewer in the center of a cake. When the skewer shows just a touch of crumbs except for the smears of melted chocolate or comes out clean, the cakes are done. Remove the pan from the oven and place on a heat-resistant surface or wire rack.

Carefully invert the brioche pans to release the cakes 3 to 4 minutes after removing them from the oven—well before they cool completely. You may have to tap each pan firmly—or even slam it—against the sheet pan to release the cake. Place on a heat-resistant surface or wire rack to cool. Immediately soak the pans to make cleaning easier.

SERVING AND STORING

Serve at room temperature either naked or with a dusting of confectioners' sugar.

Store under a cake dome at room temperature, or wrapped in plastic in the fridge for up to 1 week. To store longer, label, date, and store the plastic-wrapped cake in the freezer for up to 1 month.

Triple Lime-Chocolate Crunchy Feet

Cranberry-Lemon Pound Cake Loaded with Chocolate

> *This cake attracts crowds and won't last long, especially when it's served still warm from the oven.*

Celebrate winter flavors with the crisp blend of fresh lemon and dried cranberries. Since these ingredients are available year-round this cake is perfect for any occasion. Look for unsweetened or apple juice–sweetened dried cranberries in the bulk foods aisle at your local grocery stores. Gin may seem like an odd ingredient for a cake but it's derived in part from the pungent juniper berry, which lends a mild but distinct woodsy flavor and pairs well with the lemon. Adding the chocolate takes it to another level. The three flavors are balanced but still boldly assertive in their own right. (It's really good without chocolate, too. Just leave it out if you want it to be chocolate-free.)

EQUIPMENT: rasp or plane zester, mixing bowls, standing mixer, one 12-cup Bundt pan or small brioche pans

YIELD: one 12-cup Bundt cake or 32 Crunchy Feet

INGREDIENTS

Dry

unbleached all-purpose flour, 13 ounces (2½ cups + 1 tablespoon), *or 13½ ounces (2½ cups + 3 tablespoons) at high altitude*

dried cranberries, 3 ounces (½ cup)

bittersweet chocolate pistoles, 3 ounces (¼ cup)

potato starch, 1 tablespoon

vanilla powder, 1 tablespoon

salt, ½ teaspoon

baking soda, ¼ teaspoon

Liquid

sour cream, 4 ounces (½ cup)

half-and-half, ¾ cup, *or ¾ cup + 2 tablespoons at high altitude*

lemon, 1

gin, 2 tablespoons

vanilla extract, 1 teaspoon

Creaming

unsalted butter, at room temperature, 6 ounces (1½ sticks)

extra-fine granulated sugar, 21 ounces (2½ cups + 2 tablespoons), *or 19¾ ounces (2¼ cups + 3½ tablespoons) at high altitude*

lemon zest, 1 tablespoon

eggs (large), 5, *or 6 at high altitude*

Alcohol-free variation: Omit the gin and vanilla extract. Substitute 2 tablespoons whole milk and the seeds from ½ vanilla bean. Whisk to combine with the liquid ingredients.

PREPARE AHEAD OF TIME

1. Zest the lemon with a rasp or mince the lemon zest with a chef's knife. Set aside.

2. Segment the zested lemon (page 206).

3. Break the chocolate pistoles into small pieces with a rolling pin. If you're not using pistoles, gently break the chocolate into ¼- to ½-inch pieces, carefully chipping irregular pieces with a sharp knife. Make the pieces large enough so they'll look and taste decadent in the cake but small enough so they won't sink to the bottom of the pan. Do not melt—set aside.

1. Preheat the oven to 350°F (conventional) or 335°F (convection). Set the rack in the middle of the oven. For Crunchy Feet, set racks in the upper-middle and lower-middle positions.

2. Set out the ingredients and equipment.

• Sift the flour directly into a bowl on a scale for accurate measuring.

• Measure the other dry ingredients into a separate mixing bowl, add the flour, and whisk for 10 seconds to blend. Set aside.

• Measure the liquid ingredients into a separate bowl, whisk to combine, and set aside. Don't try to break up the lemon segments—the mixer will take care of that.

• Measure the butter and sugar into separate bowls and set aside.

• Crack the eggs into a separate bowl and set aside.

3. In the bowl of a standing mixer fitted with the paddle attachment, cream together the butter and sugar on the lowest speed for 2 to 3 minutes. The acids from the lemon zest will break down the sugar, so the creamed mixture may look a little liquid.

4. With the mixer still on the lowest speed, add the eggs one at a time, fully incorporating after each addition. Stop the mixer and scrape the sides of the bowl.

the prepared pan instead of by pouring it into one spot. Level the batter with the rubber spatula. Bake any leftover batter as Crunchy Feet or cupcakes. For Crunchy Feet, use a 2-ounce, trigger-release, ice-cream scoop to deposit the batter into the prepared pans so they're three-quarters full.

9. Follow the approximate bake times listed below.

ITEM	SEA LEVEL	HIGH ALTITUDE
12-cup Bundt	45 minutes	65 minutes
Crunchy Feet	15 minutes	30 minutes

10. Once the top of the cake doesn't jiggle in the center and looks golden brown on the edges and blonde across the top, test for doneness by inserting a bamboo skewer in the center of the cake. When the skewer shows just a touch of crumbs or comes out clean, the cake is done. Remove the pan from the oven and place on a heat-resistant surface or wire rack.

11. For Crunchy Feet, carefully invert the brioche pans to release the cakes 3 to 4 minutes after removing them from the oven—well before they cool completely. You may have to tap each pan firmly—or even slam it—against the sheet pan to release the cake. Place on a heat-resistant surface or wire rack to cool. Immediately soak the pans to make cleaning easier.

12. For the Bundt cake, once the cake has cooled for 5 to 10 minutes, remove it by inverting the pan onto a flat surface. Allow it to cool to room temperature, about 30 minutes, before glazing.

5. Add the dry ingredient mixture alternately with the liquid mixture in 3 to 5 additions each, beginning and ending with the dry mixture. Move swiftly through this step to avoid overworking the batter. Don't wait for the dry or liquid mixtures to be fully incorporated before adding the next. This step should take a total of about 60 seconds.

6. Stop the mixer and scrape the sides of the bowl all the way down. Don't miss the clumps of ingredients hiding on the bottom of the bowl. Mix on medium speed for 20 to 25 seconds to develop the batter's structure.

7. Prepare the pans. For a Bundt cake, spray the pan well with a nonstick spray. For Crunchy Feet, place the brioche pans on sheet pans (16 per half-sheet pan is a snug fit) and spray them liberally.

8. For a Bundt cake, fill the pan about three-quarters full by depositing the batter with the rubber spatula in small clumps around

SERVING AND STORING

This cake is best served right from the oven, either naked or with a dusting of confectioners' sugar. When the chocolate is still warm it oozes and drips—absolute heaven for chocoholics!

Store under a cake dome at room temperature, or wrapped in plastic in the fridge for up to 1 week. To store longer, label, date, and store the plastic-wrapped cake in the freezer for up to 1 month.

Gingerly

Fresh ginger, molasses, and Caribbean spices are long on flavor in this refreshing, light cake. It's perfect with tea or coffee, and is also one of the most popular flavors of Crunchy Feet at the bakery.

This cake calls for raw honey, a non-processed, naturally crystallized honey that is wonderfully thick. Regular honey is perfectly acceptable, but if you can find raw honey in the baking aisle of your grocery store, give it a try. It's also fantastic in hot tea.

EQUIPMENT: rasp or plane zester, mixing bowls, food processor, standing mixer, one 12-cup Bundt pan or small brioche pans

YIELD: one 12-cup Bundt cake or 32 Crunchy Feet

INGREDIENTS

Dry

unbleached all-purpose flour, 15 ounces (3 cups), *or 15½ ounces (3 cups + 1½ tablespoons) at high altitude*

cornstarch, 2 teaspoons

ground ginger, 1 teaspoon

ground cinnamon, 1 teaspoon

salt, 1 teaspoon

baking soda, ¼ teaspoon

ground allspice, ⅛ teaspoon

Liquid

sour cream, 8 ounces (1 cup)

brandy, ¼ cup

fresh ginger, about 2 inches

rum, 1 tablespoon

molasses, 1½ tablespoons

raw honey, 1 tablespoon

amaretto, 1 teaspoon

vanilla extract, 1 teaspoon

lime, 1

Creaming

unsalted butter, at room temperature, 8 ounces (2 sticks)

extra-fine granulated sugar, 20 ounces (2½ cups), *or 18¾ ounces (2¼ cups + 1½ tablespoons) at high altitude*

lime zest, 2 teaspoons

eggs (large), 6, *or 7 at high altitude*

Alcohol-free variation: Omit the brandy, rum, amaretto, and vanilla extract. Substitute 1 additional segmented lime and 2 tablespoons whole milk. Whisk to combine with the liquid ingredients.

PREPARE AHEAD OF TIME

1. Zest the lime with a rasp or mince the lime zest with a chef's knife. Set aside.

2. Segment the zested lime (page 206).

3. Peel and mince two tablespoons of fresh ginger. Mincing before processing is important—I've seen large chunks of ginger make it past the steel blade too many times.

1. Preheat the oven to 350°F (conventional) or 335°F (convection). Set the rack in the middle of the oven. For Crunchy Feet, set racks in the upper-middle and lower-middle positions.

2. Set out the ingredients and equipment.

• Sift the flour directly into a bowl on a scale for accurate measuring.

• Measure the other dry ingredients into a separate mixing bowl, add the flour, and whisk for 10 seconds to blend. Set aside.

• Measure the liquid ingredients except the lime segments into the bowl of a food processor and process for 45 seconds. Pour into a separate bowl, add the lime segments, whisk to combine, and set aside. Don't try to break up the lime segments—the mixer will take care of that.

• Measure the butter and sugar into separate bowls and set aside.

• Crack the eggs into a separate bowl and set aside.

3. In the bowl of a standing mixer fitted with the paddle attachment, cream together the butter, sugar, and lime zest on the lowest speed for 2 to 3 minutes.

4. With the mixer still on the lowest speed, add the eggs one at a time, fully incorporating after each addition. Stop the mixer and scrape the sides of the bowl.

5. Add the dry ingredient mixture alternately with the liquid mixture in 3 to 5 additions each, beginning and ending with the dry mixture. Move swiftly through this step to avoid overworking the batter. Don't wait for the dry or liquid mixtures to be fully incorporated before adding the next. This step should take a total of about 60 seconds.

6. Stop the mixer and scrape the sides of the bowl all the way down. Don't miss the clumps of ingredients hiding on the bottom of the bowl. Mix on medium speed for 15 to 20 seconds to develop the batter's structure.

7. Prepare the pans. For a Bundt cake, spray the pan well with a nonstick spray. For Crunchy Feet, place the brioche pans on sheet pans (16 per half-sheet pan is a snug fit) and spray them liberally.

8. For a Bundt cake, fill the pan about three-quarters full by depositing the batter with the rubber spatula in small clumps around the prepared pan instead of by pouring it into one spot. Level the batter with the rubber spatula. Bake any leftover batter as Crunchy Feet or cupcakes. For Crunchy Feet, use a 2-ounce, trigger-release, ice-cream scoop to deposit the batter into the prepared pans so they're three-quarters full.

9. Follow the approximate bake times listed below.

ITEM	SEA LEVEL	HIGH ALTITUDE
12-cup Bundt	50–55 minutes	60 minutes
Crunchy Feet	15 minutes	30 minutes

10. Once the top of the cake doesn't jiggle in the center and has an even, lightly browned appearance, test for doneness by inserting a bamboo skewer in the center of the cake. When the skewer shows just a touch of crumbs or comes out clean, the cake is done. Remove the pan from the oven and place on a heat-resistant surface or wire rack.

11. For Crunchy Feet, carefully invert the brioche pans to release the cakes 3 to 4 minutes after removing them from the oven—well before they cool completely. You may have to tap each pan firmly—or even slam it—against the sheet pan to release the cake. Place on a heat-resistant surface or wire rack to cool. Immediately soak the pans to make cleaning easier.

12. For the Bundt cake, once the cake has cooled for 5 to 10 minutes remove the cake by inverting the pan onto a flat surface. Allow it to cool to room temperature, about 30 minutes, before glazing.

SERVING AND STORING

Serve at room temperature either naked or with a dusting of confectioners' sugar. Don't pre-slice this cake. Something about the gingerroot dries out the cake rather quickly, despite the ample butter and sugar.

For even more flavor, pair this Bundt with rum- or lime-flavored Italian Meringue Buttercream (page 153).

Store under a cake dome at room temperature, or wrapped in plastic in the fridge for up to 1 week. If frosted, store under a cake dome for up to 3 days, or in the fridge for up to 1 week. To store unfrosted cake longer, label, date, and store the plastic-wrapped cake in the freezer for up to 1 month.

When Do I Eat
CakeLove?

I almost never have cake after eating a big meal—it just doesn't appeal to me. It's the worst thing you could do for your diet, too. The problem is the timing. Eating dessert after a big meal, especially dinner, means there's a whole lot of extra calories floating around in your body when you already have more than enough fuel to power it for the next 6 to 10 hours.

The extra calories taste good, but after dinner our body doesn't need them right away. All of those calories get stored for later use. Changing the time of day you eat cake—perhaps to midafternoon—can help you enjoy cakes much more. It'll give your body more time to metabolize what you eat instead of promptly storing it for another day.

Maple Pound Cake with Pecan Crunch Buttercream and candied pecans

Maple Pound Cake

I'm in love with pure maple syrup.

I'm in love with pure maple syrup. I always have it around for pancakes and French toast and I sneak it into dinner dishes whenever I can. My affection for it goes way back. One memory I have is when my sister Liz and I went to a firehouse pancake breakfast with our friends John and Kristin in Burton, Ohio, a tiny town way outside of Cleveland. It was one of my first visits to a pancake breakfast and I was blown away at how good everything tasted. Blueberry, banana, buckwheat, and corn pancakes were made from scratch and served with sweet cream butter and, the best part, unrestricted access to plenty of pure, fresh maple syrup. I sopped up as much syrup as I could, platter after platter after platter!

This is a rich butter cake for anyone who loves anything maple. The recipe is already packed with maple crystals but if you want even more maple flavor you can double up on them. Maple crystals can be found in the baking aisle of your grocery store or gourmet food store. The crystals vary in size—I like to use a crystal that's roughly the size of a BB.

EQUIPMENT: mixing bowls, standing mixer, one 12-cup Bundt pan or small brioche pans

YIELD: one 12-cup Bundt cake or 32 Crunchy Feet

INGREDIENTS

Dry

unbleached all-purpose flour, 13½ ounces (2½ cups + 3 tablespoons), *or 14 ounces (2¾ cups + ½ teaspoon) at high altitude*

potato starch, 1 tablespoon

vanilla powder, 1½ teaspoons

baking soda, ¼ teaspoon

salt, ½ teaspoon

maple crystals, 6 tablespoons

Liquid

sour cream, 8 ounce (1 cup)

heavy cream, 2 tablespoons, *or 2 tablespoons + 1 teaspoon at high altitude*

pure maple syrup, ⅓ cup

brandy, ¼ cup

amaretto, 1 tablespoon

rum, 1 tablespoon

vanilla extract, 1½ teaspoons

whiskey, 1 teaspoon

Creaming

unsalted butter, at room temperature, 8 ounces (2 sticks)

extra-fine granulated sugar, 18½ ounces (2¼ cups + 1 tablespoon), *or 18 ounces (2¼ cups) at high altitude*

vanilla bean, 1

eggs (large), 5, *or 6 at high altitude*

yolk (large), 1

1. Preheat the oven to 350°F (conventional) or 335°F (convection). Set the rack in the middle of the oven. For Crunchy Feet, set racks in the upper-middle and lower-middle positions.

2. Set out the ingredients and equipment.

• Sift the flour directly into a bowl on a scale for accurate measuring.

• Measure the other dry ingredients into a separate mixing bowl, add the flour, and whisk for 10 seconds to blend. Set aside.

• Measure the liquid ingredients into a separate bowl, whisk to combine, and set aside.

• Measure the butter and sugar into separate bowls and set aside.

• Crack the eggs and yolk into separate bowls and set aside.

3. In the bowl of a standing mixer fitted with the paddle attachment, cream together the butter and sugar on the lowest speed for 2 to 3 minutes.

4. Meanwhile, slice the vanilla bean lengthwise with a paring knife and scrape out the seeds. Add the seeds to the creaming butter and sugar. Reserve the pod for another use.

5. With the mixer still on the lowest speed, add the eggs one at a time followed by the yolk, fully incorporating after each addition. Stop the mixer and scrape the sides of the bowl.

6. Add the dry ingredient mixture alternately with the liquid mixture in 3 to 5 additions each, beginning and ending with the dry mixture. Don't wait for the dry or liquid mixtures to be fully incorporated before adding the next. This step should take a total of about 60 seconds.

7. Stop the mixer and scrape the sides of the bowl all the way down. Mix on medium speed for 15 to 20 seconds to develop the batter's structure.

8. Prepare the pans. For a Bundt cake, spray the pan well with a nonstick spray. For Crunchy Feet, place the brioche pans on sheet pans (16 per half-sheet pan is a snug fit) and spray them liberally.

9. For a Bundt cake, fill the pan about three-quarters full by depositing the batter with the rubber spatula in small clumps around the prepared pan. Level the batter with the rubber spatula. Bake any leftover batter as Crunchy Feet or cupcakes. For Crunchy Feet, use a 2-ounce, trigger-release, ice-cream scoop to deposit the batter into the prepared pans so they're three-quarters full.

10. Follow the approximate bake times listed below.

ITEM	SEA LEVEL	HIGH ALTITUDE
12-cup Bundt	45–50 minutes	70 minutes
Crunchy Feet	15 minutes	30 minutes

11. Once the top of the cake doesn't jiggle in the center and is blonde across the top and lightly browned around the edges, test for doneness by inserting a bamboo skewer in the center of the cake. When the skewer shows just a touch of crumbs or comes out clean, the cake is done. Remove the pan from the oven and place on a heat-resistant surface or wire rack.

12. For Crunchy Feet, carefully invert the brioche pans to release the cakes 3 to 4 minutes after removing them from the oven—well before they cool completely. You may have to tap each pan firmly—or even slam it—against the sheet pan to release the cake. Place on a heat-resistant surface or wire rack to cool. Immediately soak the pans to make cleaning easier.

13. For the Bundt cake, once the cake has cooled for 5 to 10 minutes remove the cake by inverting the pan onto a flat surface. Allow it to cool to room temperature, about 30 minutes, before glazing.

SERVING AND STORING

Serve at room temperature either naked or with a dusting of confectioners' sugar. To boost flavor and add a special touch, use Apricot Preserve Glaze (page 176), substituting pure maple syrup for the water. For total decadence, serve with Pecan Crunch Buttercream (page 164), as on page 88. (See page 200 for more information on layering and assembling.)

Store under a cake dome at room temperature, or wrapped in plastic in the fridge for up to 1 week. To store longer, label, date, and store the plastic-wrapped cake in the freezer for up to 1 month.

Slicing a vanilla bean   Scraping out the seeds   The seeds revealed

Butter
Cakes

Even though these batters are very fragile, they're worth the trouble—hot out of the oven these cakes are ridiculously soft and delicious.

All of the mixing stages for butter cakes mirror those of pound cakes (see pages 24–29), but the batter will come together much more quickly due to the smaller amounts of ingredients. There's a certain art to mixing the batter for a butter cake, and you'll master it with a little practice.

Please note one distinct difference in pan preparation for butter cakes: Don't use nonstick spray. Line the bottoms of the pans with parchment paper cut exactly to size, but don't grease the sides. The batter will cling to the nongreased surface as it rises in the oven. If the pan sides are greased, the batter slips off the slick surface and falls onto itself, resulting in a dense, short cake with a wrinkled perimeter. When the cake can "walk" up the pan sides, the edges are taller and there isn't a difference in density between the edge and the center of the cake.

I prefer to use cake pans with straight sides simply because it helps me keep the sides of the cake straight when I'm assembling a layer cake. Pans with flared sides work just as well for baking, but if you're upgrading bakeware or purchasing pans for the first time, consider pans with straight sides. They're easier to work with.

Dancing butter and sugar

Clumping to the beater

Coating the bowl

Add the eggs

Add some dry ingredients

Add some liquid ingredients

Scrape the bowl

Properly mixed batter

Deposit the batter

Level the batter

Finding
a Balance

When mixing ingredients, you don't want to be too quick or too rough, as that can deflate your batter. You also don't want to go too slowly, which will give the gluten in the flour too much time to activate and will toughen the cake. Try to walk the line between overwhelming and underwhelming the batter when adding ingredients, mixing in more of whatever is next immediately after the last item is fully incorporated, unless otherwise specified in the recipe. I wish I could say wait 5 seconds or 10 seconds, but there's no precise period to wait for any single step when mixing batter.

Guidelines for each step are given in the recipes, but they're not commandments written in stone. Many factors can affect the outcome of mixing a batter, including humidity, room temperature, and barometric pressure. When I bake, I try to understand the recipe from the inside out. I try to picture myself inside the mixing bowl and imagine I can see up close how well the ingredients are mixing. Getting the right texture, height, and taste is really about knowing when to speed up and when to slow down, just like when you're driving a car or riding a bike. Don't get discouraged—everyone can learn this.

Chocolate Butter Cake with Coconut Buttercream

Chocolate Butter Cake

Chocolate cakes that look super dark but have a disappointingly weak chocolate flavor drive me crazy—double that when they leave me with dry mouth. About two years before I opened CakeLove, I set out to develop a recipe from scratch for a rich, moist, and irresistible basic chocolate cake. Experimenting in the kitchen brings triumphs and tragedies, and a lot of people kindly helped out by sampling some tragedies before I finally created my ideal chocolate cake.

There are many things that make a chocolate cake memorable. One of the most important aspects I focus on is cocoa powder. I always use a full-fat, unsweetened, Dutch-processed cocoa powder with 22% to 24% cocoa butter—that's twice the amount of cocoa butter in common grocery-aisle cocoa powder. Regularly available unsweetened cocoa powder with 10% to 12% cocoa butter works perfectly well in this recipe, but try the other kind if you can find it. It'll make a difference.

EQUIPMENT: mixing bowls, standing mixer, two 9-inch-round pans or cupcake pans

YIELD: two 9-inch round cakes or 24 cupcakes

INGREDIENTS

Dry

unbleached all-purpose flour, 7 ounces (1¼ cups + 2 tablespoons), *or 7¼ ounces (1¼ cups + 3 tablespoons) at high altitude*

unsweetened cocoa powder, 2 ounces (½ cup), *or 2⅛ ounces (½ cup + 1 tablespoon + ½ teaspoon) at high altitude*

baking powder, 1½ teaspoons, *or 1 teaspoon at high altitude*

salt, 1 teaspoon

Liquid

half-and-half, 1 cup, *or 1 cup + 2½ tablespoons at high altitude*

brandy, 2 tablespoons

vanilla extract, 1 tablespoon

Creaming

unsalted butter, at room temperature, 6 ounces (1½ sticks)

extra-fine granulated sugar, 14 ounces (1¾ cup), *or 13 ounces (1½ cups + 2 tablespoons) at high altitude*

eggs (large), 4, *or 5 at high altitude*

Alcohol-free variation: Omit the brandy and vanilla and increase the half-and-half by 1 tablespoon.

1. Preheat the oven to 350°F (conventional) or 335°F (convection). Set the rack in the middle of the oven. For cupcakes, set racks in the upper-middle and lower-middle positions.

2. Set out the ingredients and equipment.

• Sift the flour directly into a bowl on a scale for accurate measuring.

• Measure the other dry ingredients into a separate mixing bowl, add the flour, and whisk for 10 seconds to blend. Set aside.

• Measure the liquid ingredients into a separate bowl and set aside.

• Measure the butter and sugar into separate bowls and set aside.

• Crack the eggs into a separate bowl and set aside.

3. In the bowl of a standing mixer fitted with the paddle attachment, cream together the butter and sugar on the lowest speed for 3 to 5 minutes.

4. With the mixer still on the lowest speed, add the eggs one at a time, fully incorporating after each addition. Stop the mixer and scrape the sides of the bowl.

5. Add the dry ingredient mixture alternately with the liquid mixture in 3 to 5 additions each, beginning and ending with the dry mixture. Move swiftly through this step to avoid overworking the batter. Don't wait for the dry or liquid mixtures to be fully incorporated before adding the next. This step should take a total of about 60 seconds.

6. Stop the mixer and scrape the sides of the bowl all the way down. Don't miss the clumps of ingredients hiding on the bottom of the bowl. Mix on medium speed for 15 to 20 seconds to develop the batter's structure.

7. Prepare the pans. For 9-inch-round cakes, line the bottom of each pan with parchment; do not spray the sides. For cupcakes, lightly spray the pan with a nonstick spray to help release any overflowing crowns. Line the pan with paper liners.

8. For 9-inch-round cakes, deposit the batter in three separate areas of each pan and smooth out with the rubber spatula or an offset metal spatula, making sure the pans are two-thirds full. For cupcakes, use a 2-ounce, trigger-release, ice-cream scoop to deposit batter into the lined pans so they're two-thirds full.

9. Follow the approximate bake times listed below.

ITEM	SEA LEVEL	HIGH ALTITUDE
9-inch rounds	28 minutes	35 minutes
cupcakes	22 minutes	20 minutes

10. Once the top of the cake doesn't jiggle in the center, test for doneness by inserting a bamboo skewer in the center of the cake. An even dark brown color should extend from the edge to the center, and the cake's edges may pull away from the pan. When the skewer shows just a touch of crumbs or comes out clean, the cake is done. Remove the pan from the oven and place on a heat-resistant surface or wire rack.

11. For 9-inch-round cakes, cool to room temperature, 25 to 30 minutes, before removing from the pans. Use a small offset spatula to loosen each cake from the rim of the pan. Carefully invert each pan onto a flat surface and remove the layers. Remove the parchment from the bottom of each cake and wrap the cake tightly in plastic. Refrigerate the layers for up to 5 days before frosting. (See page 200 for more information on layering and assembling.)

12. For cupcakes, cool to room temperature, 25 to 30 minutes, before carefully lifting each cupcake from the pan. Proceed with frosting or store for later use.

SERVING AND STORING

Serve frosted with your choice of buttercream (pages 150–67). It's especially good paired with Coconut Buttercream, as on page 96.

Store under a cake dome at room temperature, or wrapped in plastic in the fridge for up to 1 week. If frosted, store under a cake dome for up to 3 days, or in the fridge for up to 1 week. To store unfrosted cake longer, label, date, and store the plastic-wrapped cake in the freezer for up to 1 month.

Yellow Butter Cake

> *Don't taste this cake right out of the oven or you'll eat the whole batch!*

This perfectly flavored vanilla cake is a derivative of the Chocolate Butter Cake. I merely substitute potato starch for the cocoa powder. Like its chocolate counterpart, it has a light, buttery flavor.

The batter may look somewhat unstable, like it's separating if it sits too long before panning. Don't worry, just give the batter a few turns with a rubber spatula to bring it back together.

EQUIPMENT: mixing bowls, standing mixer, two 9-inch-round pans or cupcake pans

YIELD: two 9-inch round cakes or 24 cupcakes

INGREDIENTS

Dry

unbleached all-purpose flour, 7 ounces (1¼ cup + 2 tablespoons), *or 7¼ ounces (1¼ cup + 3 tablespoons) at high altitude*

potato starch, 2 ounces

baking powder, 1½ teaspoons, *or 1 teaspoon at high altitude*

salt, 1 teaspoon

Liquid

half-and-half, 1 cup, *or 1 cup + 2 tablespoons at high altitude*

brandy, 2 tablespoons

vanilla extract, 1 tablespoon

Creaming

unsalted butter, at room temperature, 6 ounces (1½ sticks)

extra-fine granulated sugar, 14 ounces (1¾ cups), *or 13 ounces (1½ cups + 2 tablespoons) at high altitude*

eggs (large), 4, *or 5 at high altitude*

Alcohol-free variation: Omit the brandy and vanilla and increase the half-and-half by 1 tablespoon.

1. Preheat the oven to 350°F (conventional) or 335°F (convection). Set rack in the middle of the oven. For cupcakes, set racks in the upper-middle and lower-middle positions.

2. Set out the ingredients and equipment.

• Sift the flour directly into a bowl on a scale for accurate measuring.

• Measure the other dry ingredients into a separate mixing bowl, add the flour, and whisk for 10 seconds to blend. Set aside.

• Measure the liquid ingredients into a separate bowl and set aside.

• Measure the butter and sugar into separate bowls and set aside.

• Crack the eggs into a separate bowl and set aside.

3. In the bowl of a standing mixer fitted with the paddle attachment, cream together the butter and sugar on the lowest speed for 3 to 5 minutes.

4. With the mixer still on the lowest speed, add the eggs one at a time, fully incorporating after each addition. Stop the mixer and scrape the sides of the bowl.

5. Add the dry ingredient mixture alternately with the liquid mixture in 3 to 5 additions each, beginning and ending with the dry mixture. Move swiftly through this step to avoid overworking the batter. Don't wait for the dry or liquid mixtures to be fully incorporated before adding the next. This step should take a total of about 60 seconds.

6. Stop the mixer and scrape the sides of the bowl all the way down. Don't miss the clumps of ingredients hiding on the bottom of the bowl. Mix on medium speed for 15 to 20 seconds to develop the batter's structure.

7. Prepare the pans. For 9-inch-round cakes, line the bottom of each pan with parchment; do not spray the sides. For cupcakes, lightly spray the pan with a nonstick spray to help release any overflowing crowns. Line the pan with paper liners.

8. For 9-inch-round cakes, deposit the batter in three separate areas of each pan and smooth out with the rubber spatula or an offset metal spatula, making sure the pans are two-thirds full. For cupcakes, use a 2-ounce, trigger-release, ice-cream scoop to deposit batter into the lined pans so they're two-thirds full.

9. Follow the approximate bake times listed below.

ITEM	SEA LEVEL	HIGH ALTITUDE
9-inch rounds	28 minutes	32 minutes
cupcakes	22 minutes	20 minutes

10. Once the top of the cake doesn't jiggle in the center, test for doneness by inserting a bamboo skewer in the center of the cake. The center should be an even blonde color, and the edges should be just beginning to pull away from the pan. When the skewer shows just a touch of crumbs or comes out clean, the cake is done. Remove the pan from the oven and place on a heat-resistant surface or wire rack.

11. For 9-inch-round cakes, cool to room temperature, 25 to 30 minutes, before removing from the pans. Use a small offset spatula to loosen each cake from the rim of the pan. Carefully invert each pan onto a flat surface and remove the layers. Remove the parchment from the bottom of each cake and wrap the cake tightly in plastic. Assembling a layer cake is easier if the cake is cold, so refrigerate the layers overnight or for up to 5 days before frosting.

12. For cupcakes, cool to room temperature, 25 to 30 minutes, before carefully lifting each cupcake from the pan. Proceed with frosting or store for later use.

SERVING AND STORING

Serve frosted with your choice of buttercream (pages 150–67).

Store under a cake dome at room temperature, or wrapped in plastic in the fridge for up to 1 week. If frosted, store under a cake dome for up to 3 days, or in the fridge for up to 1 week. To store unfrosted cake longer, label, date, and store the plastic-wrapped cake in the freezer for up to 1 month.

Yellow Butter Cake with raspberry-flavored Italian Meringue Buttercream and fresh raspberries

White Butter Cake

I rarely bake a white cake because I don't stock cake flour at the bakery. A lot of people prefer to use cake flour for cakes—they say it produces a finer crumb that slices more easily and melts in your mouth. In my experience, cake flour doesn't offer enough gluten for the flavor or structure I like, so they tend to crumble and taste bland.

Nevertheless, using cake flour (along with using egg whites without the yolks) is really the only way to achieve a true white cake.

This recipe makes a lot of cupcakes (30 rather than the standard 24) but the extra batter is necessary to yield two 9-inch-round cakes. If you want to make less batter, just reduce the recipe by one-third.

EQUIPMENT: mixing bowls, standing mixer, two 9-inch-round pans or cupcake pans

YIELD: two 9-inch round cakes or 30 cupcakes

INGREDIENTS

Dry

cake flour, 12 ounces (2½ cups + 2 teaspoons), *or 12½ ounces (2¾ cups + ½ teaspoon) at high altitude*

potato starch, 3 ounces

baking powder, 1½ teaspoons, *or 1 teaspoon at high altitude*

salt, ¾ teaspoon

Liquid

egg whites, ¾ cup, *or ¾ cup + 1 ½ tablespoons at high altitude*

whole milk, ¾ cup, *or ¾ cup +2 tablespoons at high altitude*

half-and-half, ¼ cup + 2 tablespoons, *or ¼ cup + 3 tablespoons at high altitude*

vanilla extract, 1½ teaspoons

Creaming

unsalted butter, at room temperature, 7½ ounces (1¾ sticks)

extra-fine granulated sugar, 18 ounces (2¼ cups), *or 17¼ ounces (2 cups + 1 ½ tablespoons) at high altitude*

vanilla bean (optional), 1

Alcohol-free variation: Omit the vanilla extract and substitute with the seeds from ¾ vanilla bean.

1. Preheat the oven to 350°F (conventional) or 335°F (convection). Set rack in the middle of the oven. For cupcakes, set racks in the upper-middle and lower-middle positions.

2. Set out the ingredients and equipment.

• Sift the flour directly into a bowl on a scale for accurate measuring.

• Measure the other dry ingredients into a separate mixing bowl, add the flour, and whisk for 10 seconds to blend. Set aside.

• Measure the liquid ingredients into a separate bowl, whisk to combine, and set aside. Whisking with the egg whites will require a bit more effort than usual to incorporate.

• Measure the butter and sugar into separate bowls and set aside.

3. In the bowl of a standing mixer fitted with the paddle attachment, cream together the butter and sugar on the lowest speed for 2 to 3 minutes. There is less sugar in this recipe than others, so the butter and sugar will take slightly longer to become light and fluffy.

4. Meanwhile, slice the vanilla bean lengthwise with a paring knife and scrape out the seeds. Add the seeds to the creaming butter and sugar. Reserve the pod for another use.

5. Add the dry ingredient mixture alternately with the liquid mixture in 3 to 5 additions each, beginning and ending with the dry mixture. Move swiftly through this step to avoid overworking the batter. Don't wait for the dry or liquid mixtures to be fully incorporated before adding the next. This step should take a total of about 60 seconds.

6. Stop the mixer and scrape the sides of the bowl all the way down. Mix on medium speed for 20 to 30 seconds to develop the batter's structure.

7. Prepare the pans. For 9-inch-round cakes, line the bottom of each pan with parchment; do not spray the sides. For cupcakes, lightly spray the pan with a nonstick spray to help release any overflowing crowns. Line the pan with paper liners.

8. For 9-inch-round cakes, deposit the batter in three separate areas of each pan and smooth out with the rubber spatula or an offset metal spatula, making sure the pans are only half full. The cakes will bake to fill most of the pan. For cupcakes, use a 2-ounce, trigger-release, ice-cream scoop to deposit batter into the lined pans so they're only half full.

Follow the approximate bake times listed below.

ITEM	SEA LEVEL	HIGH ALTITUDE
9-inch rounds	35 minutes	45 minutes
cupcakes	25 minutes	30 minutes

Once the top of the cake doesn't jiggle in the center, test for doneness by inserting a bamboo skewer in the center of the cake. The edges should be golden brown and just beginning to pull away from the sides of the pan, and the top of the cake should still look pale. When the skewer shows just a touch of crumbs or comes out clean, the cake is done. Remove the pan from the oven and place on a heat-resistant surface or wire rack.

For 9-inch-round cakes, cool to room temperature, 25 to 30 minutes, before removing from the pans. Use a small offset spatula to loosen each cake from the rim of the pan. Carefully invert each pan onto a flat surface and remove the layers. Remove the parchment from the bottom of each cake and wrap the cake tightly in plastic. Assembling a layer cake is easier if the cake is cold, so refrigerate the layers overnight or for up to 5 days before frosting.

For cupcakes, cool to room temperature, 25 to 30 minutes, before carefully lifting each cupcake from the pan. Proceed with frosting or store for later use.

SERVING AND STORING

Serve frosted with your choice of buttercream (pages 150–67).

Store under a cake dome at room temperature, or wrapped in plastic in the fridge for up to 1 week. If frosted, store under a cake dome for up to 3 days, or in the fridge for up to 1 week. To store unfrosted cake longer, label, date, and store the plastic-wrapped cake in the freezer for up to 1 month.

Cherry-Chocolate Chip Cupcakes

This cupcake is slightly sweeter than the rest, but it's loaded with chocolate. Who could ever have a problem with that?

EQUIPMENT: food processor, 2-quart, heavy-bottomed saucepan, mixing bowls, standing mixer, cupcake pans

YIELD: 16 cupcakes

INGREDIENTS

Dry

unbleached all-purpose flour, 5 ounces
(1 cup), *or 5¼ ounces (1 cup + 2 teaspoons)
at high altitude*

chopped dried cherries, 4 ounces (½ cup)

semisweet chocolate chips, 5 ounces (½ cup)

unsweetened cocoa powder, 1 ounce
(¼ cup), *or 1¼ ounces (¼ cup + 1 tablespoon) at high altitude*

baking soda, 1 teaspoon, *or ¼ teaspoon at
high altitude*

salt, ½ teaspoon

Liquid

whole milk, ½ cup, *or ½ cup + 1 tablespoon +
1 teaspoon at high altitude*

Cherry Puree (page 107), ¼ cup

vanilla extract, 1 teaspoon

Creaming

unsalted butter, at room temperature,
3 ounces (¾ stick)

extra-fine granulated sugar, 12 ounces
(1½ cups), *or 11¼ ounces (1 cup + 2 tablespoons + 2 teaspoons) at high altitude*

eggs (large), 3, *or 4 at high altitude*

yolk (large), 1

Cherry–Chocolate Chip Cupcake with cherry-flavored Italian Meringue Buttercream

Alcohol-free variation: Omit the vanilla extract and substitute the seeds from ½ vanilla bean.

PREPARE AHEAD OF TIME

1. Chop the dried cherries and chocolate chips into ¼- to ½-inch pieces with a chef's knife. Set aside.

2. Make the Cherry Puree (facing page). Measure ¼ cup and reserve the remainder for another use.

1. Preheat the oven to 350°F (conventional) or 335°F (convection). Set racks in the upper-middle and lower-middle positions.

2. Set out the ingredients and equipment.

• Sift the flour directly into a bowl on a scale for accurate measuring.

• Measure the other dry ingredients into a separate mixing bowl, add the flour, and whisk for 10 seconds to blend. Set aside.

• Measure the liquid ingredients into a separate bowl, whisk to combine, and set aside.

• Measure the butter and sugar into separate bowls and set aside.

• Crack the eggs and yolk into two separate bowls and set aside.

3. In the bowl of a standing mixer fitted with the paddle attachment, cream together the butter and sugars on the lowest speed for 2 to 3 minutes.

4. With the mixer still on the lowest speed, add the eggs one at a time followed by the yolk, fully incorporating after each addition.

5. Add the dry ingredient mixture alternately with the liquid mixture in 3 to 5 additions each, beginning and ending with the dry mixture. Move swiftly through this step to avoid overworking the batter. Don't wait for the dry or liquid mixtures to be fully incorporated before adding the next. This step should take a total of about 60 seconds.

6. Stop the mixer and scrape the sides of the bowl all the way down. Don't miss the clumps of ingredients hiding on the bottom of the bowl. Mix on medium speed for 15 to 20 seconds to develop the batter's structure.

7. Prepare the pans. Lightly spray the pans with a nonstick spray to help release any overflowing crowns. Line the pans with paper liners.

8. Using a 2-ounce, trigger-release, ice-cream scoop, deposit batter into the lined pans so they're two-thirds full.

9. Follow the approximate baking times listed below.

ITEM	SEA LEVEL	HIGH ALTITUDE
cupcakes	20 minutes	25 minutes

10. Once the tops of the cupcakes don't jiggle in the center and won't dent when poked, test for doneness by inserting a bamboo skewer in the center of a cupcake. When the skewer shows just a touch of crumbs or comes out clean, the cake is done. Remove the pan from the oven and place on a heat-resistant surface or wire rack.

11. Cool to room temperature, 25 to 30 minutes, before carefully lifting each cupcake from the pan. Proceed with frosting or store for later use.

SERVING AND STORING

Serve frosted with your choice of buttercream (pages 150–67).

Store under a cake dome at room temperature, or wrapped in plastic in the fridge for up to 1 week. If frosted, store under a cake dome for up to 3 days, or in the fridge for up to 1 week. To store unfrosted cake longer, label, date, and store the plastic-wrapped cake in the freezer for up to 1 month. To store unfrosted cake longer, label, date, and store the plastic-wrapped cake in the freezer for up to 1 month.

Cherry Puree

Whether you're using it for Cherry–Chocolate Chip Cupcakes or other cakes where you want a sweet, fruity accent, this puree is a good way to bring in the taste of cherries, which is sometimes hard to capture. Be sure to reduce the puree slowly to prevent the sugars from burning and ruining the flavor.

EQUIPMENT: 2-quart, heavy-bottomed saucepan, food processor

YIELD: about 1½ cups

INGREDIENTS
Puree
frozen cherries, one 10-ounce bag

extra-fine granulated sugar, 4 ounces (½ cup)

1. Thaw the package of frozen cherries in the bag. Do not strain the juice.

2. Place the cherries in the bowl of a food processor and puree for about 1 minute until totally smooth.

3. Transfer to a 2-quart, heavy-bottomed saucepan and add the sugar. Slowly bring to a simmer over low to medium heat and cook for 20 to 25 minutes, or until the liquid is reduced at least by half. Don't boil.

4. Remove from the heat and cool completely.

Light and Lemony Cake

This recipe uses less butter than most of the others and has a bright lemon flavor. While much of the flavor of homestyle baking comes from butter, it can also overwhelm a cake. Here I've substituted cream cheese for some of the butter. The result is a soft texture that provides a mildly tangy base for the lemon to build on.

EQUIPMENT: rasp or plane zester, mixing bowls, standing mixer, one 12-cup Bundt pan, two 9-inch-round pans, or small brioche or cupcake pans

YIELD: one 12-cup Bundt cake, two 9-inch-round cakes, 24 Crunchy Feet, or 24 cupcakes

INGREDIENTS

Dry

unbleached all-purpose flour, 8½ ounces
    (1½ cups + 3 tablespoons), *or 9 ounces*
    (1¾ cups + 1 tablespoon) at high altitude
potato starch, 2 tablespoons
salt, ½ teaspoon
baking soda, ¼ teaspoon

Liquid

lemons, 2
sour cream, ¼ cup
heavy cream, ¼ cup, *or ¼ cup + 2 teaspoons*
    at high altitude
whole milk, ¼ cup, *or ¼ cup + 2 teaspoons*
    at high altitude
limoncello, 1 tablespoon
vanilla extract, ½ teaspoon
lemon oil, ¼ teaspoon

Creaming

unsalted butter, at room temperature,
    4 ounces (1 stick)
cream cheese, 3 ounces
extra-fine granulated sugar, 16 ounces
    (2 cups), *or 15 ounces (1¾ cups +*
    2 tablespoons) at high altitude
turbinado sugar, 2 tablespoons
lemon zest, 1 tablespoon
eggs (large), 4, *or 5 at high altitude*
yolk (large), 1

Alcohol-free variation: Omit the limoncello and vanilla extract. Add the seeds from ½ vanilla bean to the creaming mixture.

PREPARE AHEAD OF TIME

1. Zest the lemon with a rasp or mince the lemon zest with a chef's knife. Set aside.
2. Segment the zested lemon (page 206).

1. Preheat the oven to 350°F (conventional) or 335°F (convection). Set rack in the middle of the oven for Bundt or layer cakes, and in the upper-middle and lower-middle for Crunchy Feet or cupcakes.

2. Set out the ingredients and equipment.

• Sift the flour directly into a bowl on a scale for accurate measuring.

• Measure the other dry ingredients into a separate mixing bowl, add the flour, and whisk for 10 seconds to blend. Set aside.

• Measure the liquid ingredients into a separate bowl, whisk to combine, and set aside. Don't try to break up the lemon segments—the mixer will take care of that.

• Measure the butter, cream cheese, sugar, and turbinado sugar into separate bowls and set aside.

• Crack the eggs and yolk into two separate bowls and set aside.

3. In the bowl of a standing mixer fitted with the paddle attachment, cream together the butter, cream cheese, sugars, and lemon zest on the lowest speed for 3 to 4 minutes.

4. With the mixer still on the lowest speed, add the eggs one at a time, fully incorporating after each addition. Stop the mixer and scrape the sides of the bowl.

5. Add the dry ingredient mixture alternately with the liquid mixture in 3 to 5 additions each, beginning and ending with the dry. Don't wait for the dry or liquid mixtures to be fully incorporated before adding the next. This step should take a total of about 60 seconds.

6. Stop the mixer and scrape the sides of the bowl all the way down. Don't miss the clumps of ingredients hiding on the bottom of the bowl. Mix on medium speed for 15 to 20 seconds.

7. Prepare the pans. For a Bundt cake, spray the pan well with a nonstick spray. For 9-inch-round cakes, line the bottom of each pan with parchment but do not spray the sides. For Crunchy Feet, place the brioche pans on sheet pans and spray liberally with a nonstick spray. For cupcakes, lightly spray the pan with a nonstick spray and line the pan with paper liners.

8. For a Bundt cake, fill the pan about three-quarters full by depositing the batter with the spatula in small clumps around the prepared pan instead of by pouring it into one spot. Level the batter with the spatula. For 9-inch-round cakes, deposit the batter in three separate areas of each pan and smooth out with a spatula, making sure the pans are two-thirds full. For Crunchy Feet or cupcakes, use a 2-ounce, trigger-release, ice-cream scoop to deposit the batter into the prepared pans so they're three-quarters full or two-thirds full, respectively.

9. Follow the approximate bake times listed below.

ITEM	SEA LEVEL	HIGH ALTITUDE
12-cup Bundt	45–50 minutes	50 minutes
9-inch rounds	30 minutes	40 minutes
Crunchy Feet	15–18 minutes	30 minutes
cupcakes	22 minutes	32 minutes

10. Once the top of the cake is a golden blonde color, insert a bamboo skewer in the center of the cake. When the skewer shows just a touch of crumbs or comes out clean, the cake is done. Remove the pan from the oven and place on a heat-resistant surface or wire rack.

11. For the Bundt cake, once the cake has cooled for 5 to 10 minutes, remove the cake by inverting the pan onto a flat surface. Allow it to cool to room temperature, about 30 minutes, before glazing.

12. For the layer cake, cool to room temperature, 25 to 30 minutes, before removing from the pan. Use a small offset spatula to loosen the cake from the rim of the pan and carefully invert onto a flat surface. Remove the parchment from the bottom and wrap the cake tightly in plastic. Refrigerate for up to 5 days before frosting.

13. For Crunchy Feet, carefully invert the brioche pans to release the cakes 3 to 4 minutes after removing them from the oven—well before they cool completely. You may have to tap each pan firmly—or even slam it—against the sheet pan to release the cake. Place on a heat-resistant surface or wire rack to cool.

14. For cupcakes, cool to room temperature, 25 to 30 minutes, before carefully lifting each cupcake from the pan. Proceed with frosting or store for later use.

SERVING AND STORING

Serve the Bundt or Crunchy Feet naked or with a dusting of confectioners' sugar. Pair the layer cake or cupcakes with vanilla- or lemon-flavored Italian Meringue Buttercream (page 153).

Store under a cake dome at room temperature, or wrapped in plastic in the fridge for up to 1 week or in the freezer for up to 1 month. If frosted, store under a cake dome for up to 3 days, or in the fridge for up to 1 week.

Mr. Banana Legs

Mr. Banana Legs is like the perfect "little black dress."

When a close friend asked for a cake with banana as the featured ingredient, I was stumped. I find banana a little tough to work with. I don't like traditional banana bread because it's usually oily and soggy. And generally speaking its flavor doesn't stand up well to the dominant flavor of flour in cake. The banana flavor in this cake won't bonk you over the head, but the cake does have a creamy banana mouthfeel and pairs well with fresh banana slices.

Porche Lovely tested these recipes at high altitude. She offered this about the cake: Mr. Banana Legs is a favorite among my tasters because they loved the texture. One ate three slices in one sitting! Pureeing the bananas with the liquid ingredients results in a lighter cake that doesn't suffer the heavy, gummy fate of banana bread. And Mr. Banana Legs is like the perfect "little black dress"—you can dress it up for more formal occasions but it's also perfect for a weekday afternoon party with friends. It's good for breakfast or dessert.

EQUIPMENT: mixing bowls, rasp, standing mixer, one 12-cup Bundt pan, two 9-inch-round pans, or small brioche pans

YIELD: one 12-cup Bundt cake, two 9-inch-round cakes, or 26 Crunchy Feet

---

INGREDIENTS

Dry

unbleached all-purpose flour, 10 ounces
   (2 cups), *or 10¾ ounces (2 cups + 2 table-*
   spoons + 1 teaspoon) at high altitude
potato starch, 1 tablespoon
turbinado sugar, 1 tablespoon
salt, ½ teaspoon
baking soda, ¼ teaspoon, *or none*
   at high altitude
whole nutmeg, 1

Liquid

very ripe peeled bananas, 6 ounces
   (3 bananas)
half-and-half, ¾ cup, *or ¾ cup +*
   2 tablespoons at high altitude
rum, 1 tablespoon
vanilla extract, 1½ teaspoons

Creaming

unsalted butter, at room temperature,
   6 ounces (1½ sticks)
extra-fine granulated sugar, 21 ounces
   (2¾ cups), *or 19½ ounces (2¼ cups +*
   3 tablespoons) at high altitude
eggs (large), 4, *or 5 at high altitude*
yolks (large), 3

Mr. Banana Legs with rum-flavored Italian Meringue Buttercream, Ganache, and fresh bananas

Alcohol-free variation: Omit the rum and vanilla extract. Substitute 2 tablespoons whole milk and the seeds from 1 vanilla bean. Whisk to combine with the liquid ingredients.

PREPARE AHEAD OF TIME

Grate the nutmeg with a rasp. Measure ⅛ teaspoon and set aside.

1. Preheat the oven to 350°F (conventional) or 335°F (convection). Set rack in the middle of the oven. To bake Crunchy Feet, place the oven racks in the upper-middle and lower-middle positions.

2. Set out the ingredients and equipment.

- Sift the flour directly into a bowl on a scale for accurate measuring.
- Measure the other dry ingredients into a separate mixing bowl, add the flour, and whisk for 10 seconds to blend. Set aside.
- Combine the liquid ingredients in a food processor and process for 30 seconds or until smooth. Place in a separate bowl and set aside.
- Measure the butter and sugar into separate bowls and set aside.
- Crack the eggs and yolks into two separate bowls and set aside.

3. In the bowl of a standing mixer fitted with the paddle attachment, cream together the butter and sugar on the lowest speed for 2 to 3 minutes. The mixture should look white, fluffy, and aerated.

4. With the mixer still on the lowest speed, add the eggs one at a time followed by the yolks, fully incorporating after each addition. Stop the mixer and scrape the sides of the bowl.

5. Add the dry ingredient mixture alternately with the liquid mixture in 3 to 5 additions each, beginning and ending with the dry mixture. Move swiftly through this step to avoid overworking the batter. Don't wait for the dry or liquid mixtures to be fully incorporated before adding the next. This step should take a total of about 60 seconds.

6. Stop the mixer and scrape the sides of the bowl all the way down. Don't miss the clumps of ingredients hiding on the bottom of the bowl. Mix on medium speed for 15 to 20 seconds to develop the batter's structure.

7. Prepare the pans. For a Bundt cake, spray the pan well with a nonstick spray. For 9-inch-round cakes, line the bottom of each pan with parchment but do not spray the sides. For Crunchy Feet, place the brioche pans on sheet pans (16 per half-sheet pan is a snug fit) and spray them liberally with a nonstick spray.

8. For a Bundt cake, fill the pan about three-quarters full by depositing the batter with the rubber spatula in small clumps around the prepared pan instead of by pouring it into one spot. Level the batter with the rubber spatula. Bake any leftover batter as Crunchy Feet or cupcakes. For 9-inch-round cakes, deposit the batter into three separate areas of the pan and smooth out with an offset spatula, making sure the pans are two-thirds full. For Crunchy Feet, use a 2-ounce, trigger-release, ice-cream scoop to deposit the batter into the prepared pans so they're three-quarters full.

9. Follow the approximate bake times listed below.

ITEM	SEA LEVEL	HIGH ALTITUDE
12-cup Bundt	45 minutes	55 minutes
9-inch rounds	26-28 minutes	42 minutes
Crunchy Feet	15 minutes	32 minutes

10. Once the top of the cake doesn't jiggle in the center and is golden brown across the top and edges, test for doneness by inserting a bamboo skewer in the center of the cake. When the skewer shows just a touch of crumbs or comes out clean, the cake is done. Remove the pan from the oven and place on a heat-resistant surface or wire rack.

11. For the Bundt cake, once the cake has cooled for 5 to 10 minutes, remove the cake by inverting the pan onto a flat surface. Allow it to cool to room temperature, about 30 minutes, before glazing.

12. For Crunchy Feet, carefully invert the brioche pans to release the cakes 3 to 4 minutes after removing them from the oven—well before they cool completely. You may have to tap each pan firmly—or even slam it—against the sheet pan to release the cake. Place on a heat-resistant surface or wire rack to cool. Immediately soak the pans to make cleaning easier.

13. For the layer cake, cool to room temperature, 25 to 30 minutes, before removing from the pan. Use a small offset spatula to loosen the cake from the rim of the pan. Carefully invert each pan onto a flat surface·to remove the layers. Remove the parchment from the bottom of each cake and wrap the cake tightly in plastic. Assembling a layer cake is easier if the cake is cold, so refrigerate the layers overnight or for up to 5 days before frosting.

SERVING AND STORING

Serve naked or with a dusting of confectioners' sugar or use Glazing Chocolate (page 174). For a dressed-up version, serve assembled with rum-flavored Italian Meringue Buttercream (page 153), Ganache (page 172), and fresh bananas, as on page 111. (See page 200 for more information on layering and assembling.)

Store under a cake dome at room temperature, or wrapped in plastic in the fridge for up to 1 week. If frosted, store under a cake dome for up to 3 days, or in the fridge for up to 1 week. To store unfrosted cake longer, label, date, and store the plastic-wrapped cake in the freezer for up to 1 month.

Tres Leches Butter Cake

> *I had my first tres leches cake in Los Angeles when I worked as a health educator in the San Fernando Valley.*

Tres leches (Spanish for "three milks") cake is a traditional Mexican cake that has a creamy texture and a wonderfully sweet stickiness to it. The combination of evaporated milk, heavy cream, and a post-bake soaking of sweetened condensed milk creates a very rich and decidedly wet sponge for this cake. It's perfect for eating with a spoon.

Take it a step further and make this cake even more outrageous by using cajeta, a sweetened condensed milk cooked slowly to the point of caramelization so that it becomes thick like butter. Spread it onto the cake before frosting. Look for cajeta in the ethnic food section of your grocery or specialty food store.

EQUIPMENT: mixing bowls, standing mixer, two 9-inch-round pans

YIELD: two 9-inch-round cakes

INGREDIENTS

Dry

unbleached all-purpose flour, 10 ounces (2 cups)

potato starch, ¼ cup

baking powder, ½ teaspoon

salt, ½ teaspoon

cinnamon, ¼ teaspoon

Liquid

evaporated milk, ¾ cup

heavy cream, 2 tablespoons

dark rum, 2 tablespoons

vanilla extract, 1 teaspoon

Creaming

unsalted butter, at room temperature, 4 ounces (1 stick)

extra-fine granulated sugar, 8 ounces (1 cup)

confectioners' sugar, 3 ounces (¾ cup)

dark muscovado or dark brown sugar, 1 tablespoon, packed

turbinado sugar, 2 tablespoons

eggs (large), 4

Post-bake Soaking

sweetened condensed milk, ½ cup

Alcohol-free variation Omit the rum and vanilla and substitute the seeds fom 1 vanilla bean.

1. Preheat the oven to 350°F (conventional) or 335°F (convection). Set rack in the middle of the oven.

2. Set out the ingredients and equipment.

• Sift the flour directly into a bowl on a scale for accurate measuring.

• Measure the other dry ingredients into a separate mixing bowl, add the flour, and whisk for 10 seconds to blend. Set aside.

• Measure the liquid ingredients into a separate bowl, and set aside.

• Measure the butter and sugar into separate bowls and set aside.

• Crack the eggs into a separate bowl and set aside.

3. In the bowl of a standing mixer fitted with the paddle attachment, cream together the butter and sugars on the lowest speed for 2 to 3 minutes. The combination of sugars works air into the butter quickly.

4. With the mixer still on the lowest speed, add the eggs one at a time, fully incorporating after each addition. Stop the mixer and scrape the sides of the bowl.

5. Add the dry ingredient mixture alternately with the liquid mixture in 3 to 5 additions each, beginning and ending with the dry mixture. Move swiftly through this step to avoid overworking the batter. Don't wait for the dry or liquid mixtures to be fully incorporated before adding the next. This step should take a total of about 60 seconds.

6. Stop the mixer and scrape the sides of the bowl all the way down. Don't miss the clumps of ingredients hiding on the bottom of the bowl. Mix on medium speed for 15 to 20 seconds to develop the batter's structure.

7. Prepare the pans. Line the bottom of each pan with parchment; do not spray the sides.

8. Deposit the batter in three separate areas of each pan and smooth out with the rubber spatula or an offset metal spatula, making sure the pans are half full.

9. Follow the approximate bake times listed below.

ITEM	SEA LEVEL	HIGH ALTITUDE
9-inch rounds	24 minutes	34 minutes

10. Once the top of the cake doesn't jiggle in the center and the edges are golden brown and beginning to pull away from the sides of the pan, test for doneness by inserting a bamboo skewer in the center of the cake. When the skewer shows just a touch of crumbs or comes out clean, the cake is done. Remove the pan from the oven and place on a heat-resistant surface or wire rack.

11. Poke up to 50 holes in each cake with a bamboo skewer. Pour up to ¼ cup sweetened condensed milk onto each cake. Let the milk run down into the holes, gently working it into the cake with a pastry brush. Repeat until all the milk is absorbed.

12. Cool the cakes to room temperature, 25 to 30 minutes, before removing from the pan. Use a small offset spatula to loosen the cake from the rim of the pan. Carefully invert each pan onto a flat surface to remove the layers. Remove the parchment from the bottom of each cake and wrap the cake tightly in plastic. Assembling a layer cake is easier if the cake is cold, so refrigerate the layers overnight or for up to 5 days before frosting.

SERVING AND STORING

Seven-Minute Meringue Frosting (page 168) goes best with this cake. Generously slather it onto the cake, adding lots of peaks for a dramatic finish.

Store under a cake dome at room temperature, or wrapped in plastic in the fridge for up to 1 week. If frosted, store under a cake dome for up to 3 days, or in the fridge for up to 1 week. To store unfrosted cake longer, label, date, and store the plastic-wrapped cake in the freezer for up to 1 month.

Maizing

> *It may seem unusual to combine chocolate with corn, but I was inspired by the traditional Mayan and Aztec beverage made of chocolate, corn, water, and spices.*

Maizing is one of my favorites from the early days of CakeLove. We don't make it at the bakery anymore, but I love baking it at home, especially for brunch on the weekend. The combination of corn in the batter and chocolate in the frosting is amazing.

Try to serve this cake on the same day it's baked and don't refrigerate or freeze it. The corn kernels harden irreversibly when they get cold, which ruins the texture of this surprise ingredient. Frozen corn kernels that are thawed and drained are a fine substitute for fresh kernels.

EQUIPMENT: mixing bowls, standing mixer, 9-inch-round pan, 8-inch oven-safe skillet, small brioche pans, or cupcake pans

YIELD: one 9-inch-round cake, one 8-inch skillet cake, or 12 to 15 Crunchy Feet or cupcakes

INGREDIENTS

Dry

unbleached all-purpose flour, 4 ounces (¾ cup + ½ teaspoon), *or 4 ounces + ⅛ ounces (¾ cup + ½ teaspoon) at high altitude*

confectioners' sugar, 2 ounces (7 tablespoons)

cornmeal, ¼ cup

vanilla powder, 1 teaspoon

baking powder, 1 teaspoon, *or ½ teaspoon + ⅛ teaspoon at high altitude*

salt, ½ teaspoon

Liquid

half-and-half, ½ cup, *or ½ cup + 2 teaspoons at high altitude*

eggs (large), 5, *or 6 at high altitude*

yolk (large), 1

Sauté

unsalted butter, at room temperature, 2½ ounces (5 tablespoons)

fresh corn, 1 ear (½ to ¾ cup kernels)

PREPARE AHEAD OF TIME

If you're using fresh corn on the cob, shuck the corn, carefully cut the kernels off of the ear, and set aside.

1. Preheat the oven to 350°F (conventional) or 335°F (convection). Set the rack in the middle of the oven for round layer or skillet cakes. For Crunchy Feet or cupcakes, set racks in the upper-middle and lower-middle positions.

2. Set out the ingredients and equipment.

• Sift the flour directly into a bowl on a scale for accurate measuring.

• Measure the other dry ingredients into a large mixing bowl, add the flour, and whisk for 10 seconds to blend. Set aside.

• Measure the liquid ingredients into a separate bowl, whisk to combine, and set aside.

3. In an 8-inch oven-safe skillet over medium heat, melt the butter and add the corn kernels. Lightly sauté for 2 to 3 minutes, or until the kernels are slightly translucent and browned on the edges. They will begin to pop at about the same time. Remove from the heat and leave the kernels in the skillet.

4. Whisk the liquid ingredients into the dry until fully combined, about 15–20 seconds.

5. With a heat-resistant rubber spatula, gently fold the sautéed corn and the butter into the batter. Set the skillet aside if you are making the skillet cake, but do not clean it.

6. Prepare the pans. For a 9-inch-round cake, line the bottom of each pan with parchment but do not spray the sides. For Crunchy Feet, place the brioche pans on sheet pans (16 per half-sheet pan is a snug fit) and spray them liberally with a nonstick spray. For cupcakes, lightly spray the pan with a nonstick spray to help release any overflowing crowns. Line the pan with paper liners.

7. For a 9-inch round cake, deposit the batter into three separate areas of the pan and smooth out with a rubber spatula, making sure the pan is two-thirds full. For Crunchy Feet, use a 2-ounce, trigger-release, ice-cream scoop to deposit the batter into the prepared pans so they're three-quarters full. For cupcakes, use a 2-ounce, trigger-release, ice-cream scoop to deposit batter into the lined pans so they're two-thirds full. For a skillet cake, pour the batter into the sauté skillet and level the batter with an offset or rubber spatula.

8. Follow the approximate bake times listed below.

ITEM	SEA LEVEL	HIGH ALTITUDE
9-inch round	25 minutes	30 minutes
8-inch skillet cake	25 minutes	35 minutes
Crunchy Feet	15 minutes	24 minutes
cupcakes	15 minutes	20 minutes

9. Once the top of the cake appears dry and doesn't jiggle in the center, test for doneness by inserting a bamboo skewer in the center of the cake. The color should be a pale golden yellow. When the skewer shows just a touch of crumbs or comes out clean, the cake is done. Remove the pan from the oven and place on a heat-resistant surface or wire rack.

10. For the skillet cake, slice into wedges and serve warm.

11. For the 9-inch-round cake, allow it to cool slightly 5 to 10 minutes in the pan. Use a small offset spatula to loosen the cake from the rim of the pan and carefully invert it onto a cardboard cake circle or flat plate. Remove the parchment paper from the bottom. Return the cake to the wire rack or leave it on the plate to cool completely, 25 to 30 minutes, before frosting and glazing.

12. For Crunchy Feet, carefully invert the brioche pans to release the cakes 3 to 4 minutes after removing them from the oven—well before they cool completely. You may have to tap each pan firmly—or even slam it—against the sheet pan to release the cake. Place on a heat-resistant surface or wire rack to cool. Immediately soak the pans to make cleaning easier.

13. For cupcakes, carefully lift each cupcake from the pan and serve warm.

SERVING AND STORING

Serve the Crunchy Feet or cupcakes naked. Serve the skillet cake piping hot out of the oven with a dollop of your favorite honey on top—watch it melt and ooze into the cake. Serve the 9-inch-round cake assembled with Chocolate Buttercream (page 154) and covered in Ganache (page 172). (See page 200 for more information on layering and assembling.)

Store under a cake dome at room temperature, or wrapped in plastic in the fridge for up to 1 week. If frosted, store under a cake dome for up to 3 days, or in the fridge for up to 1 week. To store unfrosted cake longer, label, date, and store the plastic-wrapped cake in the freezer for up to 1 month.

No-Mixer Cakes

made without a mixer

You can mix each of these cake batters in under five minutes. It's buttery, delicious, and made without a mixer anywhere in sight! Baking from scratch has never been easier.

EQUIPMENT: mixing bowl, plastic container with lid, fine-mesh sieve, two 9-inch round pans

YIELD: two 9-inch round cakes

INGREDIENTS
Dry

unbleached all-purpose flour, 7 ounces
   (1⅓ cups), *or 7¼ ounces (1½ cups) at
   high altitude*

extra-fine granulated sugar, 12 ounces
   (1½ cups), *or 11¼ ounces (1 cup + 2
   tablespoons + 2 teaspoons) at high altitude*

confectioners' sugar, 2 ounces (¾ cup), *or
   1¾ ounces (½ cup) at high altitude*

baking powder, 1 tablespoon, *or 2 teaspoons
   at high altitude*

salt, ½ teaspoon

Liquid

unsalted butter, melted 6 ounces (1½ sticks)

whole milk, 1 cup, *or 1 cup + 2 tablespoons at
   high altitude*

heavy cream, 1 tablespoon, *or 1 tablespoon +
   1 teaspoon at high altitude*

vanilla extract, 2 teaspoons

eggs (large), 4, *or 5 at high altitude*

egg yolks (large), 1

VARIATIONS
Adjust the dry ingredients as directed.

CHOCOLATE

unsweetened cocoa powder, add 1 ounce
   (¼ cup), *or 1¼ ounces (5 tablespoons +
   1 teaspoon) at high altitude*

SPICE

unbleached all-purpose flour, add 1 ounce
   (2½ tablespoons)

salt, add ¼ teaspoon

allspice, add ½ teaspoon

ginger, add ½ teaspoon

cinnamon, add ⅛ teaspoon

extra-fine granulated sugar, subtract 4
   ounces (½ cup)

1. Preheat the oven to 350°F (conventional) or 335°F (convection). Set rack in the middle of the oven.

2. Set out the ingredients and equipment.

• Sift the flour into a bowl for accurate measurement and whisk in the other dry ingredients to combine.

• Measure the liquid ingredients into the plastic container. Seal it and shake well.

3. Whisk the liquid ingredients into the dry ingredients, combining thoroughly.

4. Prepare the pans. Line the bottom of each pan with parchment paper but do not spray the sides.

5. Equally divide the batter between the prepared pans, and bake for 25 minutes.

6. Remove the pans from the oven when the cake is golden brown and a wooden skewer poked in the center comes out clean. Cool thoroughly on a heat-resistant surface.

7. Run a thin metal spatula around the rim of the pan to release the cake, and invert onto a plate.

You did it! Serve with a dusting of powdered sugar.

Ingredients

Combine the dry ingredients

Combine the liquid ingredients

Shake well

Whisk the liquid into the dry ingredients

Deposit the batter into the parchment-lined pan

Foam Cakes

Light and airy, these cakes love to complement rather than take center stage.

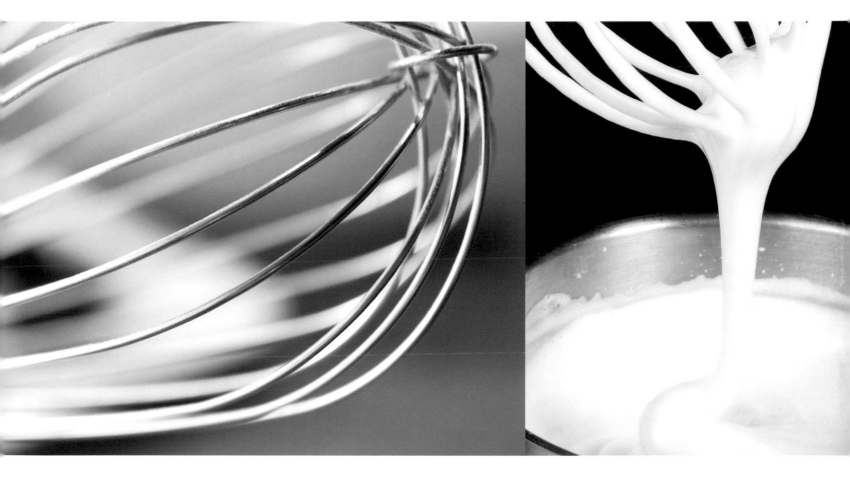

The name for this style of cake is not sexy, but it helps describe how it's made: by whipping air into egg whites, egg yolks, or both, and folding in the other ingredients. Sponge, genoise, chiffon, and soufflés are all styles of foam cakes. Foam cakes are a bit more complicated than pound cakes or butter cakes but they're easy enough to make once you get the hang of it. I think they open up a whole new dimension of texture and flavor that creamed cakes just don't have.

Two main differences distinguish foam cakes from creamed cakes: the equipment and the speed used to drive air into the batter, and the ingredients that act as the mitt to catch the air. In creamed cakes, a flat paddle revolves slowly to push sugar and air into soft butter. In foam cakes, a wire whip revolves very quickly to push air and sugar into egg whites, egg yolks, or whole eggs.

With foam cakes, if the ingredients are combined out of order the batter will be flat and will never capture air. For example, when egg whites are whipped there cannot be any fat in the bowl or on the wire whip. Fat fiercely inhibits the foaming of a meringue. The same applies to whipping egg yolks and sugar. If butter is added the whole base will collapse. So it's important to add the ingredients in proper sequence.

Foam cakes are light and airy. They frequently don't have much fat and the number of air pockets in the batter makes the cake's sponge ideal for absorbing flavored sugar syrups. Whether paired with buttercream or flavored whipped creams, the following recipes offer a nice change of flavor and texture from the pound cakes and butter cakes.

Aromatic ingredients

Whip eggs until tripled in volume

Sugar and egg foam

Preparing to fold in dry ingredients

Fold in the dry ingredients

Fold in the butter

Deposit the batter

Baked cakes reveal splotches of brown sugar

Yellow Sponge Cake (Genoise)

While sponge cake is not my favorite because it's a tad on the bland side, it's essential for everyone's cake-baking repertoires. For times when you want a lighter cake texture, or when you're using one of the heavier buttercreams (any of the nut-crunch buttercreams) and want to balance it with a lighter cake, this sponge is the one to use. No ingredient adjustments are necessary for baking at high altitude, but the baking times do differ.

EQUIPMENT: standing mixer, two 9-inch-round pans, small saucepan

YIELD: two 9-inch-round cakes

INGREDIENTS

Foam
eggs (large), 8
yolk (large), 1
extra-fine granulated sugar, 8 ounces (1 cup)

Dry
unbleached all-purpose flour, 7 ounces
 (1¼ cups + 2 tablespoons)
potato starch, ¼ cup

Liquid
unsalted butter, melted, 2 ounces (½ stick)
vanilla extract, 2 teaspoons

Alcohol-free variation: Omit the vanilla extract.

1. Preheat the oven to 350°F (conventional) or 335°F (convection). Set the rack in the middle of the oven.

2. Set out the ingredients and equipment.

• Crack the eggs and yolk into the bowl of a standing mixer fitted with the wire whip attachment.

• Measure the sugar into a bowl and set aside.

• Sift the flour directly into a bowl on a scale for accurate measuring.

• Measure the potato starch into a separate mixing bowl, add the flour, and whisk for 10 seconds to blend. Set aside.

• Measure the liquid ingredients into a separate bowl, whisk to combine, and set aside.

3. Add the sugar to the eggs and yolk and whip on high speed until a thick ribbon is formed, about 4 to 5 minutes.

4. Reduce the mixer speed to medium for about 30 seconds to stabilize the foam. Stop the mixer and remove the bowl.

5. Using a large spoon, gently sprinkle a third of the dry ingredients evenly over the top of the foam and fold in with a rubber spatula. Repeat in two more additions until the dry ingredients are fully incorporated. This step should take a total of about 30 seconds.

6. Slowly fold in the liquid ingredients just until combined.

7. Prepare the pans. Line the bottom of each pan with parchment but do not spray the sides.

8. Divide the batter equally between the prepared pans by depositing the batter into three separate areas of each pan and smoothing it out with the rubber spatula or an offset metal spatula.

9. Follow the approximate baking times listed below.

ITEM	SEA LEVEL	HIGH ALTITUDE
9-inch rounds	18 minutes	32 minutes

10. Once the tops of the cakes appear smooth and dry, don't dent when touched, and are a golden color, test for doneness by inserting a bamboo skewer in the center of a cake. When the skewer comes out clean, the cake is done. Remove the pans from the oven and place on a heat-resistant surface or wire rack.

11. Cool to room temperature, 25 to 30 minutes, before removing from the pans. Use a small offset spatula to loosen each cake from the rim of the pan. Place a cardboard cake circle or a flat plate over the pan and invert. Remove the parchment from the bottom. Assemble immediately or wrap the cakes tightly in plastic and store.

SERVING AND STORING

Serve frosted with your choice of buttercream (pages 150–67).

Store under a cake dome at room temperature, or wrapped in plastic in the fridge, for up to 1 week. If frosted, store under a cake dome for up to 3 days, or in the fridge for up to 1 week. To store unfrosted cake longer, label, date, and store the plastic-wrapped cake in the freezer for up to 2 weeks.

Curb Unnecessary Fat

A few years before I started baking I dated someone who hated fat. No butter, no olive oil, I couldn't even get grapeseed oil past her. She couldn't stand the flavor or the sensation of it. I changed my cooking techniques to accommodate her and I'm glad I did. Almost immediately I noticed that fat interferes with flavor. When fat overloads the rest of the ingredients my taste buds can't get to the flavors. It's like there's an oil slick all over my tongue and the good nubs of flavor in each ingredient slide on by.

The trouble is that cake without fat is just bread. In moderation fat adds flavor, softens the texture, and says, "I'm your decadence." But too much fat blocks the flavor of everything else in the cake and ruins the texture. Keeping the fat to a bare minimum while achieving the right texture and optimum flavor is one of the challenges I enjoy. Good cake should max out the decadent ingredients without going over the edge.

Even though I live by the motto that nothing is fat free, I try to bake cakes that are not too sweet and not too heavy. Anything else is just not sustainable for our bodies. Through trial and error and a good deal of taste-testing, finding just the right amount of fat to include was one of my first steps to building this collection of recipes.

Chocolate Sponge Cake

I created this cake one Thanksgiving morning. It's a little tradition of mine to bake something new at the original bakery on Thanksgiving. It's one of the few days we're closed and I enjoy the unusual quietness when I'm alone in the shop. When it's silent in there, it reminds me of the time before the shop opened, back when the whole idea was a dream.

The texture of this cake is very light and slightly on the dry side. It's perfect for soaking with a flavored Sugar Syrup (page 210) and layering with Basic Whipped Cream (page 169) or Seven-Minute Meringue Frosting (page 168). No ingredient adjustments are necessary for baking at high altitude, but the baking times do differ.

EQUIPMENT: standing mixer, two 9-inch-round pans

YIELD: two 9-inch-round cakes

INGREDIENTS

Foam
eggs (large), 8

yolks (large), 4

extra-fine granulated sugar, 8 ounces (1 cup)

Dry
unbleached all-purpose flour, 8 ounces
  (1½ cups + 3 tablespoons)

unsweetened cocoa powder, 1 ounce (¼ cup)

kosher salt, ¼ teaspoon

baking powder, ¼ teaspoon

confectioners' sugar, 1½ ounces
  (3 tablespoons)

vanilla powder, 1 tablespoon

Liquid
unsalted butter, melted, 1½ ounces
  (3 tablespoons)

whiskey, 2 tablespoons

Chocolate Sponge Cake with Chocolate Buttercream

Alcohol-free variation: Omit the whiskey.

1. Preheat the oven to 350°F (conventional) or 335°F (convection). Set the rack in the middle of the oven.

2. Set out the ingredients and equipment.

• Crack the eggs and yolks into the bowl of a standing mixer fitted with the wire whip attachment and set aside.

• Measure the sugar into a bowl and set aside.

• Sift the flour directly into a bowl on a scale for accurate measuring.

• Measure the other dry ingredients into a separate mixing bowl, add the flour, and whisk for 10 seconds to blend. Set aside.

• Measure the liquid ingredients into a separate bowl, whisk to combine, and set aside.

3. Add the sugar to the eggs and yolks and whip on high speed until a thick ribbon is formed, about 4 to 5 minutes.

4. Reduce the mixer speed to medium for about 30 seconds to stabilize the foam. Stop the mixer and remove the bowl.

5. Using a large spoon, gently sprinkle a third of the dry ingredients evenly over the top of the foam and fold in with a rubber spatula. Repeat in two more additions until the dry ingredients are fully incorporated. This step should take a total of about 30 seconds.

6. Slowly fold in the liquid ingredients just until combined.

7. Prepare the pans. Line the bottom of each pan with parchment but do not spray the sides.

8. Divide the batter equally between the prepared pans by depositing the batter into three separate areas of each pan and smoothing it out with the rubber spatula or an offset metal spatula.

9. Follow the approximate baking times listed below.

ITEM	SEA LEVEL	HIGH ALTITUDE
9-inch rounds	20 minutes	34 minutes

10. Once the tops of the cakes appear smooth, dry, don't dent when touched, and are even in color, test for doneness by inserting a bamboo skewer in the center of a cake. When the skewer comes out clean, the cake is done. Remove the pans from the oven and place on a heat-resistant surface or wire rack.

11. Cool to room temperature, 25 to 30 minutes, before removing from the pans. Use a small offset spatula to loosen each cake from the rim of the pan. Place a cardboard cake circle or a flat plate over the pan and invert. Remove the parchment from the bottom. Assemble immediately or wrap the cakes tightly in plastic and store. (See page 200 for more information on layering and assembling.)

SERVING AND STORING

Serve frosted with your choice of buttercream (pages 150–67).

Store under a cake dome at room temperature, or wrapped in plastic in the fridge, for up to 1 week. If frosted, store under a cake dome for up to 3 days, or in the fridge for up to 1 week. To store unfrosted cake longer, label, date, and store the plastic-wrapped cake in the freezer for up to 2 weeks.

Hazelnut Spice Sponge Cake

> I created this cake for me—I'm into mace and nutmeg more than the average person.

Here's an example of where I put aside convention for convenience. This sponge cake is supported by a touch of baking powder. Using it definitely violates the tradition of foam cakes, but it's insurance against batter deflation. I'd rather be safe than sorry.

I buy hazelnuts already blanched and skinned. They're much easier to work with than raw hazelnuts. I've tried roasting and skinning hazelnuts myself—and I won't do it again. It's time consuming, a lot of work, and hard to get right. To intensify the flavor of blanched hazelnuts, toast them on a sheet pan in a 350°F oven for 8 to 10 minutes, or until they're golden brown. Watch them closely because they will turn from perfectly golden to burned very quickly. A good rule of thumb is to remove them from the oven when they begin to smell good. No ingredient adjustments are necessary for baking at high altitude, but the baking times do differ.

EQUIPMENT: food processor, rasp, standing mixer, mixing bowls, two 9-inch-round pans

YIELD: two 9-inch-round cakes

INGREDIENTS

Foam
eggs (large), 8
yolk (large), 1
extra-fine granulated sugar, 8 ounces (1 cup)

Dry
unbleached all-purpose flour, 8 ounces
 (1½ cups + 3 tablespoons)
potato starch, 2 ounces
hazelnut powder (page 63), 4 ounces
dark brown sugar, 1 tablespoon
whole nutmeg, 1
ground mace, ½ teaspoon
kosher salt, ½ teaspoon
baking powder, ¼ teaspoon
ground allspice, ¼ teaspoon

Liquid
unsalted butter, melted, 2 ounces (½ stick)
whiskey, 2 tablespoons

PREPARE AHEAD OF TIME

1. Make the hazelnut powder (page 63). Measure 4 ounces and reserve the remainder for another use.

2. Grate the nutmeg with a rasp. Measure 1½ teaspoons and set aside.

1. Preheat the oven to 350°F (conventional) or 335°F (convection). Set the rack in the middle of the oven.

2. Set out the ingredients and equipment.

• Crack the eggs and yolk into the bowl of a standing mixer fitted with the wire whip attachment.

• Measure the sugar into a bowl and set aside.

• Sift the flour directly into a bowl on a scale for accurate measuring.

• Measure the other dry ingredients into a separate mixing bowl, add the flour, and whisk for 10 seconds to blend. Set aside.

• Measure the liquid ingredients into a separate bowl, whisk to combine, and set aside.

3. Add the sugar to the eggs and yolk and whip on high speed until a thick ribbon is formed, about 4 to 5 minutes.

4. Reduce the mixer speed to medium for about 30 seconds to stabilize the foam. Stop the mixer and remove the bowl.

5. Using a large spoon, gently sprinkle a third of the dry ingredients evenly over the top of the foam and fold in with a rubber spatula. Repeat in two more additions until the dry ingredients are fully incorporated. This step should take a total of about 30 seconds.

6. Slowly fold in the liquid ingredients just until combined.

7. Prepare the pans. Line the bottom of each pan with parchment but do not spray the sides.

8. Divide the batter equally between the prepared pans by depositing the batter into three separate areas of each pan and smoothing it out with the rubber spatula or an offset metal spatula.

9. Follow the approximate baking times listed below.

ITEM	SEA LEVEL	HIGH ALTITUDE
9-inch rounds	22–25 minutes	27 minutes

10. Once the tops of the cakes appear smooth, dry, don't dent when touched, and are blonde and uniform in color, test for doneness by inserting a bamboo skewer in the center of a cake. When the skewer comes out clean, the cake is done. Remove the pans from the oven and place on a heat-resistant surface or wire rack.

11. Cool to room temperature, 25 to 30 minutes, before removing from the pans. Use a small offset spatula to loosen each cake from the rim of the pan. Place a cardboard cake circle or a flat plate over the pan and invert. Remove the parchment from the bottom. Assemble immediately or wrap the cakes tightly in plastic and store.

SERVING AND STORING

Serve frosted with your choice of buttercream (pages 150–67).

Store under a cake dome at room temperature, or wrapped in plastic in the fridge, for up to 1 week. If frosted, store under a cake dome for up to 3 days, or in the fridge for up to 1 week. To store unfrosted cake longer, label, date, and store the plastic-wrapped cake in the freezer for up to 2 weeks.

Cinnamon and Cream Layer Cake

Inspired in part by the need for a cool, light cake for summer, I created this torte to blend cinnamon's mild bite with a soft whipped cream lightly sweetened with honey. The dense texture of the cake is designed to offset the airiness of the whipped cream sandwiched between each layer. Sampled alone the sponge tastes more like a light bread than a cake. Slice each layer ultra thin and moisten well with a rum-flavored syrup during assembly.

Because the soufflé cake is stabilized by incorporating cornstarch into the meringue, you won't have to rush when mixing. But don't lollygag either before adding the liquid ingredients!

EQUIPMENT: mixing bowls, standing mixer, two 9-inch-round pans

YIELD: two 9-inch-round cakes

INGREDIENTS

Dry

unbleached all-purpose flour, 6 ounces
   (1 cup + 3 tablespoons)

potato starch, 2 ounces

ground cinnamon, 1½ teaspoons

salt, ½ teaspoon

baking powder, ¼ teaspoon

Liquid

unsalted butter, melted, 2 ounces (½ stick)

heavy cream, 2 tablespoons

vanilla extract, 1 teaspoon

Meringue

egg whites (large), 7

extra-fine granulated sugar, 1 ounce
   (2 tablespoons)

cornstarch, 1 tablespoon

Yolk Base

yolks (large), 6

extra-fine granulated sugar, 8 ounces (1 cup)

1. Preheat the oven to 350°F (conventional) or 335°F (convection). Set the rack in the middle of the oven.

2. Set out the ingredients and equipment.

• Sift the flour directly into a bowl on a scale for accurate measuring.

• Measure the other dry ingredients into a separate mixing bowl, add the flour, and whisk for 10 seconds to blend. Set aside.

• Measure the liquid ingredients into a separate bowl, whisk to combine, and set aside.

• Separate the egg whites and yolks into two separate bowls and set aside.

• Measure the sugar and cornstarch for the meringue into a separate bowl, whisk to combine, and set aside.

3. In the bowl of a standing mixer fitted with the whip attachment, whip the egg whites on high speed until stiff peaks are formed, about 2 minutes (1½ minutes at high altitude).

4. With the mixer still on high speed, slowly add the sugar-cornstarch mixture and whip for about 15 seconds. Reduce the speed to medium for about 15 seconds to stabilize the meringue. Stop the mixer and transfer the meringue to a clean bowl. Tap the wire whip on the side of the bowl to remove all the meringue.

5. To make the yolk base, reattach the bowl and wire whip to the mixer (there's no need to clean the bowl or whip). Add the yolks and sugar and whip on high speed until the mixture is pale yellow, tripled in volume, and a thick ribbon is formed, 4 to 5 minutes.

6. With the mixer on the lowest speed, add the dry and liquid mixtures in 3 to 5 additions each, beginning and ending with the dry mixture. Move swiftly through this step to avoid overworking the batter. Don't wait for the dry or liquid mixtures to be fully incorporated before adding the next. This step should take a total of about 30 seconds.

7. With the mixer still on the lowest speed, add a third of the meringue and mix until just combined.

8. Stop the mixer and remove the bowl. Using a rubber spatula, gently fold in the remaining meringue in 2 additions until the meringue is fully incorporated.

9. Prepare the pans. Line the bottom of each pan with parchment but do not spray the sides.

10. Divide the batter equally between the prepared pans by depositing the batter into three separate areas of each pan and smoothing it out with the rubber spatula or an offset metal spatula.

11. Follow the approximate baking times listed below.

ITEM	SEA LEVEL	HIGH ALTITUDE
9-inch rounds	18 minutes	30 minutes

12. Once the tops of the cakes appear smooth, dry, and almost taupe, test for doneness by inserting a bamboo skewer in the center of each cake. When the skewer comes out clean, the cake is done. Remove the pans from the oven and place on a heat-resistant surface or wire rack.

13. Cool to room temperature, 25 to 30 minutes, before removing from the pans. Use a small offset spatula to loosen each cake from the rim of the pan. Place a cardboard cake circle or a flat plate over the pan and invert. Remove the parchment from the bottom. Assemble immediately or wrap the cakes tightly in plastic and store.

SERVING AND STORING

Assemble using rum-flavored Sugar Syrup (page 210) and Whipped Cream with Honey (page 170). (See page 200 for more information on layering and assembling.)

Store under a cake dome at room temperature for only 2 to 3 hours. To store longer, lightly cover the cake in plastic. Wrap and store in the fridge for up to 3 days.

Cinnamon

Most spices are dried ripened berries, roots, or seeds. Cinnamon is different. It's a tree bark taken from an evergreen tree, the *Cinnamomum zeylanicum* (originally from Ceylon, a region of Sri Lanka, but now cultivated in other countries). The bark is very thin and curls up when air-dried. Then it's pulverized into a powder. When you are shopping for spices, be aware that many spice companies trading in the U.S. market label *Cinnamomum cassia* (commonly known as cassia) as cinnamon. Cassia is good, but it doesn't have the delicate, sweet flavor of true cinnamon. I prefer a pungent Vietnamese-grown variety with 8% cinnamon oil.

Chocolate Pecan Bundt

This is one of those recipes that hits home with me.

I enjoyed sharing this cake with my neighbor's mother when CakeLove was just a budding idea. Before I left my job as a lawyer, I pushed myself over the edge and simply ran out of energy one night. My limbs felt like lead weights and I called for help. My neighbor Karen drove me to the hospital emergency room to get checked out and the doctor said, "You're exhausted. Slow down. You're not fifteen anymore." That was the wake-up call that permanently derailed me from the lawyer career track. When my neighbor's mother visited, she'd come upstairs to say hello and make sure I wasn't having any more episodes of exhaustion. I first shared this cake with her.

EQUIPMENT: mixing bowls, standing mixer, one 12-cup Bundt pan

YIELD: one 12-cup Bundt cake

INGREDIENTS

Dry

pecan powder (page 63), 4 ounces

unbleached all-purpose flour, 3½ ounces
   (½ cup + 2½ tablespoons)

unsweetened cocoa powder, 1½ ounces

potato starch, 1 tablespoon

baking powder, ½ teaspoon, *or ¼ teaspoon +
   ⅛ teaspoon at high altitude*

salt, ¼ teaspoon

Liquid

unsalted butter, melted, 2 ounces (½ stick)

Meringue

egg whites (large), 4

extra-fine granulated sugar, 1 ounce
   (2 tablespoons)

Yolk Base

yolks (large), 6

extra-fine granulated sugar, 6 ounces (¾ cup)

buttermilk, 4 ounces (½ cup)

PREPARE AHEAD OF TIME

Make the pecan powder (page 63). Measure 4 ounces and reserve the remainder for another use.

1. Preheat the oven to 350°F (conventional) or 335°F (convection). Set the rack in the middle of the oven.

2. Set out the ingredients and equipment.

• Sift the flour directly into a bowl on a scale for accurate measuring.

• Measure the other dry ingredients into a separate mixing bowl, add the flour, and whisk for 10 seconds to blend. Set aside.

• Separate the egg whites and yolks into two separate bowls and set aside.

• Measure the sugar for the meringue and the yolk base into two separate bowls.

• Measure the buttermilk into a separate bowl and set aside.

3. In the bowl of a standing mixer fitted with the whip attachment, whip the egg whites on high speed until stiff peaks are formed, about 2 minutes (1½ minutes at high altitude).

4. With the mixer still on high speed, slowly add the 2 tablespoons sugar and whip for 10 seconds to incorporate. Stop the mixer and transfer the meringue to a clean bowl. Tap the wire whip on the side of the bowl to remove all the meringue.

5. To make the yolk base, reattach the bowl and wire whip to the mixer (there's no need to clean the bowl or whip). Add the yolks and sugar and whip on high speed until the mixture is pale yellow, tripled in volume, and a thick ribbon is formed, about 3 minutes.

6. With the mixer on medium speed, drizzle in the buttermilk.

7. Reduce the mixer speed to low and add the dry ingredients in 3 additions, fully incorporating after each addition, followed by a third of the meringue. The batter will look dry and crumbly.

8. Stop the mixer and remove the bowl. Using a rubber spatula, gently fold in the remaining meringue in 2 additions until the meringue is fully incorporated.

9. Fold the melted butter into the batter with the rubber spatula. Stop when the batter appears smooth and the color is uniformly brown.

10. Spray the pan well with a nonstick spray.

11. Fill the pan about three-quarters full by depositing the batter with the rubber spatula in small clumps around the prepared pan instead of by pouring it into one spot. Level the batter with the rubber spatula.

12. Follow the approximate bake times listed below.

ITEM	SEA LEVEL	HIGH ALTITUDE
12-cup Bundt	40–45 minutes	40 minutes

13. Once the top of the cake doesn't jiggle in the center and looks smooth, dry, and has an rich, even, dark brown color, test for doneness by inserting a bamboo skewer in the center of the cake. When the skewer shows just a touch of crumbs or comes out clean, the cake is done. Remove the pan from the oven and place on a heat-resistant surface or wire rack.

14. Once the cake has cooled for 15 to 20 minutes, remove the cake by inverting the pan onto a flat surface. Allow it to cool to room temperature, about 40 minutes.

SERVING AND STORING

Serve with Whipped Cream with Honey (page 170).

Store under a cake dome at room temperature, or wrapped in plastic in the fridge, for up to 1 week. If frosted, store under a cake dome for up to 3 days, or in the fridge for up to 1 week. To store unfrosted cake longer, label, date, and store the plastic-wrapped cake in the freezer for up to 2 weeks.

Black Forest Cake

This Black Forest Cake doesn't look or taste like the black forest cakes found in most bakeries in the United States. The recipe is closely adapted from that of the mother-in-law of one of my customers, who lives in Germany. I was asked to bake this for her wedding, in the traditional style and method. I had to improvise a little because I couldn't read the recipe—it was in German!

This recipe calls for bittersweet chocolate pieces chopped off a large block. The irregular shapes create a unique flavor and texture in the finished cake.

EQUIPMENT: mixing bowls, standing mixer, two 9-inch round pans

YIELD: two 9-inch-round cakes

INGREDIENTS

Dry

unbleached all-purpose flour, 6 ounces
(1 cup + 3 tablespoons)

potato starch, 1 tablespoon

unsweetened cocoa powder, 1 teaspoon

salt, ¼ teaspoon

baking powder, ½ teaspoon, *or ¼ teaspoon*
+ ⅛ teaspoon at high altitude

bittersweet chocolate, chopped, 3 ounces
(⅔ cup)

Liquid

heavy cream, ¼ cup

unsalted butter, melted, 2 ounces (½ stick)

vanilla extract, 2 teaspoons

Meringue

egg whites (large), 9

extra-fine granulated sugar, 4 ounces (½ cup)

Yolk Base

yolks (large), 6

extra-fine granulated sugar, 6 ounces
(¾ cup)

Black Forest Cake with Soured Dried Cherries and Whipped Cream with Cinnamon

1. Preheat the oven to 350°F (conventional) or 335°F (convection). Set the rack in the middle of the oven.

2. Set out the ingredients and equipment.

• Sift the flour directly into a bowl on a scale for accurate measuring.

• Measure the other dry ingredients into a separate mixing bowl, add the flour, and whisk for 10 seconds to blend. Set aside.

• Measure the liquid ingredients into a separate bowl, whisk to combine, and set aside.

• Separate the egg whites and yolks into two separate bowls and set aside.

• Measure the sugar for the meringue and yolk base into two separate bowls.

3. In the bowl of a standing mixer fitted with the whip attachment, whip the egg whites on high speed until stiff peaks are formed, about 3 minutes (2½ minutes at high altitude).

4. With the mixer still on high speed, slowly add the 2 tablespoons sugar and whip for about 15 seconds to incorporate. Reduce the speed to medium for about 15 seconds to stabilize the meringue. Stop the mixer, transfer the meringue to a clean bowl, and set aside for no more than 5 minutes.

5. To make the yolk base, reattach the bowl and wire whip to the mixer (there's no need to clean the bowl or whip). Add the yolks and sugar and whip on high speed until the mixture is pale yellow, tripled in volume, and a thick ribbon is formed, 4 to 5 minutes.

6. With the mixer on the lowest speed, add the dry and liquid mixtures in 3 to 5 additions each, beginning and ending with the dry mixture. Move swiftly through this step to avoid overworking the batter. Don't wait for the dry or liquid mixtures to be fully incorporated before adding the next. This step should take a total of about 30 seconds.

7. With the mixer still on the lowest speed, add a third of the meringue and mix until just combined.

8. Stop the mixer and remove the bowl. Using a rubber spatula, gently fold in the remaining meringue in 2 additions until the meringue is fully incorporated.

9. Prepare the pans. Line the bottom of each pan with parchment but do not spray the sides.

10. Divide the batter equally between the prepared pans by depositing the batter into three separate areas of each pan and smoothing it out with the rubber spatula or an offset metal spatula.

11. Follow the approximate baking times listed below.

ITEM	SEA LEVEL	HIGH ALTITUDE
9-inch rounds	18 minutes	35 minutes

12. Once the tops of the cakes look smooth and dry, test for doneness by inserting a bamboo skewer in the center of each cake. When the skewer comes out clean, the cake is done. Remove the pans from the oven and place on a heat-resistant surface or wire rack.

13. Cool to room temperature, 25 to 30 minutes, before removing from the pans. Use a small offset spatula to loosen each cake from the rim of the pan. Place a cardboard cake circle or a flat plate over the pan and invert. Remove the parchment from the bottom. Assemble immediately or wrap the cakes tightly in plastic and store.

SERVING AND STORING

As on page 139, assemble by brushing each layer with cherry brandy–flavored Sugar Syrup (page 210), frosting with Whipped Cream with Cinnamon (page 171), and dotting each frosted layer with Soured Dried Cherries (page 213). (See page 200 for more information on layering and assembling.)

Store under a cake dome at room temperature, or wrapped in plastic in the fridge, for up to 1 week. If frosted, store under a cake dome for up to 3 days, or in the fridge for up to 1 week. To store unfrosted cake longer, label, date, and store the plastic-wrapped cake in the freezer for up to 2 weeks.

'Da Mocha!

Somehow this cake tastes like cookies-and-cream ice cream. That's a good thing—and a mystery I don't try to solve.

Coffee and chocolate come together in this foam cake that tastes like a pound cake but is butter free. Mildly agitated cream and half-and-half trap enough air when whipped with sugar to give the cake height and a soft texture. There will be "tunnels," or long air pockets, in the cake which normally indicate too much baking powder or uncontrolled gluten development. During my early days of baking I toyed with using cream instead of butter to tame the gluten in flour while adding an extra dose of liquid to the batter. It works well, especially in chocolate cakes that tend to taste dry. The holes are somewhat distracting, but I don't mind because I like the flavor that comes from using cream instead of butter.

EQUIPMENT: mixing bowls, standing mixer, one 12-cup Bundt pan

YIELD: one 12-cup Bundt cake

INGREDIENTS

Whipping

heavy cream, 1¼ cups, *or 1¼ cups + 3 tablespoons at high altitude*

half-and-half, ¾ cup, *or ¾ cup + 2 tablespoons at high altitude*

extra-fine granulated sugar, 16 ounces (2 cups), *or 15 ounces (1¾ cups + 2 tablespoons) at high altitude*

eggs (large), 4, *or 5 at high altitude*

yolks (large), 2

Dry

unbleached all-purpose flour, 11 ounces (2 cups + 3 tablespoons), *or 11½ ounces (2½ cups) at high altitude*

unsweetened cocoa powder, 2 ounces (½ cup)

confectioners' sugar, 5 ounces (1¼ cups), *or 4¾ ounces (1 cup + 2 tablespoons) at high altitude*

freshly ground espresso (finest grind), ¼ cup

cocoa nibs, 2 tablespoons

baking powder, 2 teaspoons, *or 1¼ teaspoons at high altitude*

vanilla powder, ½ teaspoon

salt, ½ teaspoon

ground allspice, ¼ teaspoon

Liquid

sour cream, 2 tablespoons

vanilla extract, 1 teaspoon

molasses, 1 teaspoon

1. Preheat the oven to 350°F (conventional) or 335°F (convection). Set the rack in the middle of the oven.

2. Set out the ingredients and equipment.

• Sift the flour directly into a bowl on a scale for accurate measuring. Using a clean bowl, do the same with the confectioners' sugar.

• Measure the other dry ingredients into a separate mixing bowl, add the flour and confectioners' sugar, and whisk for 10 seconds to blend. Set aside.

• Measure the liquid ingredients into a separate bowl, whisk to combine, and set aside.

• Crack the eggs and yolks into two separate bowls and set aside.

• Measure the heavy cream, half-and-half, and sugar into the bowl of a standing mixer fitted with the wire whip attachment.

3. Whip the cream, half-and-half and sugar mixture on medium-high speed for 30 to 45 seconds, until the combination thickens a bit.

4. Reduce the mixer speed to low and add the eggs, one at a time, followed by the yolks one at a time, fully incorporating after each addition.

5. Stop the mixer, remove the wire whip, and attach the flat paddle. With the mixer on medium speed, add the dry ingredient mixture alternately with the liquid mixture in 3 to 4 additions each, beginning and ending with the dry mixture. Move swiftly through this step to avoid overworking the batter. Don't wait for the dry or liquid mixtures to be fully incorporated before adding the next. This step should take a total of about 60 seconds.

6. Stop the mixer and scrape the sides of the bowl all the way down. Don't miss the clumps of ingredients hiding on the bottom of the bowl. Mix on medium speed for 15 to 20 seconds to develop the batter's structure.

7. Spray the pan well with a nonstick spray.

8. Fill the prepared pan about three-quarters full. Even though this batter is a bit runny compared to the others, don't pour the batter into one spot and let it ooze around the pan. Instead, deposit the batter with the rubber spatula in small clumps around the pan.

9. Follow the approximate bake times listed below.

ITEM	SEA LEVEL	HIGH ALTITUDE
12-cup Bundt	40–45 minutes	60 minutes

10. Once the top of the cake doesn't jiggle in the center but still glistens, test for doneness by inserting a bamboo skewer in the center of the cake. When the skewer shows just a touch of crumbs or comes out clean, the cake is done. Remove the pan from the oven and place on a heat-resistant surface or wire rack.

11. Once the cake has cooled for 5 to 10 minutes, remove the cake by inverting the pan onto a flat surface. Allow it to cool to room temperature, about 30 minutes, before glazing.

SERVING AND STORING

Soak this cake with a heavy dousing of Home-Brewed Espresso Syrup (page 211). For a special presentation, garnish with chocolate-covered espresso beans, which you can purchase at your favorite coffee store, and sprinkle with confectioners' sugar (as on facing page).

Keep this Bundt wrapped in plastic and under a cake dome at room temperature for up to 3 days. The lack of butter will make the cake dry out more quickly than other cakes.

'Da Mocha with chocolate-covered espresso beans and confectioners' sugar

Chocolate Soufflé Bundt

> *The texture of this cake is so delicate that the scribble in my original notes simply says "very soft."*

I adore the deep flavor and dark color of this cake I created during my first months of experimenting. I brought slices of the first version of this cake with me on a plane ride from Washington, DC to Los Angeles. I shared some with the flight attendants and the passengers sitting next to me. I can't even remember what we talked about, but I remember that it was fun. Cake is magic.

This recipe uses a partially cooked meringue to deliver moisture and an exceptionally delicate texture to the cake. It's a soufflé cake that won't grow tall like traditional soufflés because the proteins in the meringue have been cooked, or fixed, by the hot sugar syrup.

EQUIPMENT: 2-quart, heavy-bottomed saucepan, mixing bowls, standing mixer, 12-cup Bundt pan

YIELD: one 12-cup Bundt cake

INGREDIENTS
Meringue
egg whites (large), 7
extra-fine granulated sugar, 8 ounces (1 cup)
water, ¼ cup

Yolk Base
egg yolks (large), 4
confectioners' sugar, 4¼ ounces (1 cup)
heavy cream, 2 cups
vanilla extract, 1 teaspoon

Dry
unbleached all-purpose flour, 9 ounces
  (1½ cups + 3 tablespoons)
unsweetened cocoa powder, 3 ounces
  (¾ cup)
potato starch, 1½ ounces (¼ cup)
vanilla powder, ½ teaspoon
baking powder, 1 tablespoon + ½ teaspoon,
  or 2 teaspoons at high altitude
salt, ½ teaspoon

Alcohol-free variation: Omit the vanilla extract and substitute the seeds from 1 vanilla bean. Whisk to combine with the yolk base.

1. Preheat the oven to 350°F (conventional) or 335°F (convection). Set the rack in the middle of the oven.

2. Set out the ingredients and equipment.
- Separate the egg whites and yolks into two separate bowls.
- Measure the sugar and water for the meringue into two separates bowls.
- Measure the confectioners' sugar, heavy cream, and vanilla extract into a medium-sized bowl, whisk to combine, and set aside.
- Sift the flour directly into a bowl on a scale for accurate measuring.
- Measure the other dry ingredients into a separate mixing bowl, add the flour, and whisk for 10 seconds to blend. Set aside.

3. To make the stabilized meringue, combine the 1 cup of sugar and the water in a 2-quart, heavy-bottomed saucepan over medium-high heat and heat to 230°F. Meanwhile, in the bowl of a standing mixer fitted with the wire whip attachment, whip the egg whites on high speed until stiff peaks form. Keep the mixer running and, when the syrup is at 230°F, slowly pour it into the meringue. Continue whipping for about 30 seconds to fully distribute the heat from the syrup so it cooks the meringue. Stop the mixer and transfer the meringue to a clean bowl and set aside.

4. To make the yolk base, reattach the bowl and wire whip to the mixer (there's no need to clean the bowl or whip). Add the egg yolks and cream mixture and whip on medium speed until the mixture thickens slightly and shows some body, about 1 minute.

5. Stop the mixer, remove the wire whip, and attach the paddle. With the mixer on the lowest speed, add the dry ingredient mixture in 3 additions followed by a third of the meringue. The batter will look dry and crumbly.

6. Stop the mixer and remove the bowl. Using a rubber spatula, fold in the remaining meringue in 2 additions until the batter appears smooth and the color is uniformly brown.

7. Spray the pan well with a nonstick spray.

8. Fill the prepared pan about three-quarters full by depositing the batter with the rubber spatula in small clumps around the prepared pan instead of by pouring it into one spot. Level the batter with the rubber spatula.

9. Follow the approximate bake times listed below.

ITEM	SEA LEVEL	HIGH ALTITUDE
12-cup Bundt	50–55 minutes	55 minutes

10. Once the top of the cake doesn't jiggle in the center but still glistens, test for doneness by inserting a bamboo skewer in the center of the cake. When the skewer shows just a touch of crumbs or comes out clean, the cake is done. Remove the pan from the oven and place on a heat-resistant surface or wire rack.

11. Once the cake has cooled for 5 to 10 minutes, remove the cake by inverting the pan onto a flat surface. Allow it to cool to room temperature, about 30 minutes, before glazing.

SERVING AND STORAGE

Soak this cake with a citrus-flavored Sugar Syrup (page 210). For a special presentation, decorate with long strands of lemon or orange zest—a nice contrast against the dark chocolate Bundt. Alternatively, drown it in Ganache (page 172).

Store under a cake dome at room temperature, or wrapped in plastic in the fridge, for up to 1 week. If frosted, store under a cake dome for up to 3 days, or in the fridge for up to 1 week. To store unfrosted cake longer, label, date, and store the plastic-wrapped cake in the freezer for up to 2 weeks.

Coconut-Pineapple Crunchy Feet

> *It's like a piña colada on a plate!*

This is a recipe I developed for Stompin' Grounds, a coffee shop on Capitol Hill and my first regular client. While developing this recipe for them, I discovered that there's a lot of oil in coconut—even dried. After some trial and error, I realized that there is really enough oil in the dried coconut to act as the shortening in this cake. I treated it like a nut and combined it with confectioners' sugar in a one-to-one ratio. Only a little butter was necessary, and mostly just for flavor.

EQUIPMENT: mixing bowls, food processor, standing mixer, small brioche pans

YIELD: 26 Crunchy Feet

INGREDIENTS

Meringue

egg whites (large), 6, *or 7 at high altitude*

extra-fine granulated sugar, 2 tablespoons

Yolk Base

yolks (large), 8, *or 9 at high altitude*

extra-fine granulated sugar, 16 ounces (2 cups), *or 15 ounces (1¾ cups + 2 tablespoons) at high altitude*

Dry

unbleached all-purpose flour, 10 ounces (2 cups), *or 10½ ounces (2 cups + 1½ tablespoons) at high altitude*

coconut powder (instructions below), 8 ounces

cornstarch, 2 tablespoons

salt, ½ teaspoon

baking soda, ¼ teaspoon

dried pineapple, 10 ounces

Liquid

sour cream, 8 ounces (1 cup)

coconut rum, 2 tablespoons

dark rum, 2 tablespoons

unsalted butter, melted, 1 ounce (¼ stick)

vanilla extract, 1 teaspoon

limoncello, 1 teaspoon

PREPARE AHEAD OF TIME

Make the coconut powder. Combine 4 ounces unsweetened coconut chips and 4 ounces confectioners' sugar in the bowl of a food processor and process into a fine powder, 20 to 30 seconds. Set aside.

1. Preheat the oven to 335°F (conventional) or 325°F (convection). Set racks in the upper-middle and lower-middle positions.

2. Set out the ingredients and equipment.

• Sift the flour directly into a bowl on a scale for accurate measuring.

• Measure the other dry ingredients, except the pineapple, into a separate mixing bowl, add the flour and the coconut powder, and whisk for 10 seconds to blend. Set aside.

• Combine the pineapple and 2 tablespoons of the dry ingredients in the bowl of a food processor and pulse 3 times for 3 seconds each, or until the pineapple is reduced to ¼-inch chunks. Whisk into the dry ingredients.

• Measure the liquid ingredients into a separate bowl, whisk to combine, and set aside.

• Separate the egg whites and yolks into two separate bowls and set aside.

• Measure the sugar for the meringue and the yolk base into two separate bowls.

3. In the bowl of a standing mixer fitted with the wire whip attachment, whip the egg whites on high speed until stiff peaks are formed, about 2 minutes (1½ minutes at high altitude). Add the two tablespoons sugar and whip for another 15 seconds. Stop the mixer and transfer the meringue to a clean bowl and set aside.

4. To make the yolk base, reattach the bowl back on the mixer. (There's no need to clean the bowl or whip.) Add the yolks and sugar and whip on high speed until the mixture is pale yellow, tripled in volume, and a thick ribbon is formed, 4 to 5 minutes (3 minutes at high altitude). Stop the mixer, remove the wire whip, and attach the paddle.

5. With the mixer on the lowest speed, add the dry and liquid mixtures in 3 to 5 additions each, beginning and ending with the dry mixture. Move swiftly through this step to avoid overworking the batter. Don't wait for the dry or liquid mixtures to be fully incorporated before adding the next. This step should take a total of about 30 seconds.

6. With the mixer still on the lowest speed, add a third of the meringue and mix until just combined.

7. Stop the mixer and remove the bowl. Using a rubber spatula, gently fold in the remaining meringue in 2 additions until the meringue is fully incorporated.

8. Prepare the pans. Place the brioche pans on sheet pans (16 per half-sheet pan is a snug fit) and spray them liberally with a nonstick spray.

9. Using a 2-ounce, trigger-release, ice-cream scoop, deposit the batter into the prepared pans so they're three-quarters full.

10. Follow the approximate bake times listed below.

ITEM	SEA LEVEL	HIGH ALTITUDE
Crunchy Feet	15 minutes	30 minutes

11. Once the tops of the cakes look smooth and dry and golden in color with browned edges, test for doneness by inserting a bamboo skewer in the center of a cake. When the skewer shows just a touch of crumbs or comes out clean, the cake is done. Remove the pans from the oven and place on a heat-resistant surface or wire rack.

12. Carefully invert the brioche pans to release the cakes 3 to 4 minutes after removing them from the oven—well before they cool completely. The dried pineapple loves to stay attached to the pans and removing the cakes while they're still hot is really the only surefire way to get them out of the pans. You may have to tap each pan firmly—or even slam it—against the sheet pan to release the cake. Place on a heat-resistant surface or wire rack to cool. Immediately soak the pans to make cleaning easier.

SERVING AND STORING

Serve immediately or store under a cake dome at room temperature and serve within 24 hours. Due to the low butter content these cakes will dry out more quickly than most cakes.

Frostings
and Glazes

A good frosting is what cake is all about.
Made right, it'll make everyone weak at the knees.

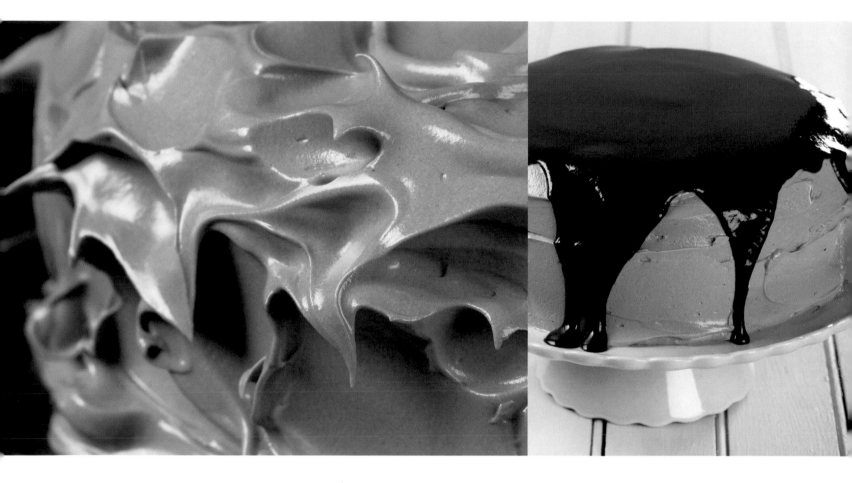

When I first started baking I had no idea what buttercream was. I was really in the dark about it. When a friend of mine said, "There's nothing like a homemade buttercream," I just muttered "Uh-huh," and kept the conversation going.

Intrigued but doubtful that it was as good as she suggested, I gave it a shot a few days later for her friend's birthday cake. I thought the recipe would read: add cream to the butter and combine with sugar. Boy, was I wrong! There were only a few ingredients in the recipe but the flavor was so complex—not too sweet, rich but light, similar to custard and whipped cream, but not tasting like either one. I was instantly hooked. I have a lot of fun with buttercreams so I hope you'll enjoy them too. I've learned that there are a lot of different buttercreams that exist in the world of baking. What's included on the following pages are the buttercreams that I love to make, whether at the bakery, for my friends, or at home for my family.

At first glance buttercreams seem trickier than they really are. When I first read that I had to pour a hot syrup into the mixer while it was running on high speed, I immediately thought the author was out of his mind. What if the syrup goes astray, hits the revolving wire whip, and flies into my eye? Thankfully nothing like that has ever happened because pouring hot sugar syrup into a standing mixer is a breeze.

For a lot of people buttercream is what cake is all about. Making different types or sticking with one and adding flavors to customize it is part of the joy in baking. Each recipe requires a slightly different method, so please read the directions all the way through before you begin. The step-by-step photos will assist you in mastering the essential points in each process.

Yellow Butter Cake cupcake with raspberry-flavored Italian Meringue Buttercream

Italian Meringue Buttercream

This is the standard buttercream at CakeLove. It has a smooth texture, it's easy to work with, and one recipe is enough for a three- or four-layer 9-inch cake. It's rich, so a little goes a long way. I like this buttercream because it has an excellent taste profile, is versatile and easy to flavor, and handles well when decorating.

Timing is important when making the cooked meringue that is the base for this buttercream. Be sure to heat the sugar syrup to 245°F before pouring it into the egg whites that have been whipped to stiff peaks. (Hint: Begin heating the syrup before you begin whipping the egg whites. Bringing the sugar syrup to 245°F usually takes about twice as long as whipping the egg whites to stiff peaks.) When the syrup is this hot the proteins in the meringue cook thoroughly and accommodate the butter. Traditional recipes for this style of buttercream cue the baker to pour the syrup when it's at 242°F. I like to raise the temperature just a little higher because the syrup will cool a little during pouring. If the syrup's temperature is lower than 245°F, the final buttercream can be too soft to hold its shape and structure when spreading onto a cake.

I always use a candy thermometer to test whether the syrup is hot enough; it's safe, practical, and accurate. Most candy thermometers are a little top heavy, so placing it with the numbers facing away from you may help it stay put in the saucepan.

EQUIPMENT: standing mixer, 1-quart heavy-bottom saucepan, candy thermometer

YIELD: 4 to 5 cups (enough for one 9-inch-round three-layer cake or 24 cupcakes)

INGREDIENTS
Buttercream
egg whites (large), 5
extra-fine granulated sugar, 10 ounces (1¼ cups)
cold water, ¼ cup
unsalted butter (at room temperature), 1 pound (4 sticks)

Ingredients

Sugar syrup

Whip the egg whites

Pour in ¼ cup sugar

Add the syrup slowly

Whip until cool, then add the butter

1. Set out the ingredients and equipment.

• Separate the egg whites into the bowl of a standing mixer fitted with the wire whip attachment.

• Measure 1 cup sugar and the water into a 1-quart, heavy-bottomed saucepan. Gently stir to combine (I use the candy thermometer for this).

• Measure the remaining ¼ cup sugar into a small bowl and set aside.

• Cut the butter into tablespoon-sized pieces and set aside in a medium bowl.

2. To make the sugar syrup, place the candy thermometer in the saucepan and heat the mixture over medium-high heat. Partially cover with a lid to capture the evaporating water—this helps to moisten the sides of the saucepan to prevent sugar crystals from forming.

3. With the mixer on high speed, begin whipping the egg whites to stiff peaks. When the peaks are stiff, you have a meringue.

4. Keep the mixer running and pour the ¼ cup of sugar into the meringue.

5. Raise the heat under the sugar syrup to bring the syrup to 245°F, if it is not there already. When the syrup is at 245°F, remove the thermometer and slowly pour the syrup into the meringue.

6. After 1 to 2 minutes reduce the mixer speed to medium for 3 to 4 minutes, or until the meringue is cooled. Add the butter 1 tablespoon at a time. Increase the mixer speed to high for 1 to 2 minutes, or until the butter is fully incorporated.

Flavor
Variations

The following flavorings can be added to the base recipe for Italian Meringue Buttercream.

FLAVOR	INGREDIENT	AMOUNT
vanilla	vanilla extract	1 teaspoon
chocolate	bittersweet chocolate, melted	½ cup
rum	dark rum	2 to 4 tablespoons (to taste)
amaretto	amaretto	2 to 4 tablespoons (to taste)
raspberry	raspberry puree	¼ to ½ cup
lemon	limoncello	2 tablespoons
orange	orange oil	1 teaspoon
lime	lime oil	1 teaspoon

Chocolate Buttercream

This is related to the nut-crunch family of buttercreams (pages 161–67), but it's chocolate all the way through. It's smooth, dark, and intense. It's also best made when the temperature is cool and the humidity is low. When there's too much moisture in the air, this type of buttercream tends not to behave well.

This recipe gives the adventurous baker the option to incorporate cocoa nibs to deepen the flavor and add texture. Cocoa nibs are small pieces of unprocessed cocoa beans. They have an earthy flavor, add crunch, and when covered in chocolate they taste even better. Look for them at your gourmet supply shop or search for them online (see Resources, page 218).

EQUIPMENT: mixing bowls, 2-quart, heavy-bottomed saucepan, standing mixer

YIELD: 4 to 5 cups (enough for one 9-inch-round, three-layer cake or 24 cupcakes)

INGREDIENTS

Yolk Mixture

yolks (large), 6

extra-fine granulated sugar, 2 ounces (¼ cup)

potato starch, 2 tablespoons

unsweetened cocoa powder, 3 tablespoons

Milk Mixture

whole milk, 2 cups

extra-fine granulated sugar, 12 ounces (1½ cups)

Flavorings and Butter

unsalted butter, chilled, 1 pound (4 sticks)

vanilla extract, 2 teaspoons

chocolate-covered cocoa nibs (optional), 2 tablespoons

1. Set out the ingredients and equipment.

• Separate the yolks into a large bowl. Add the 2 ounces sugar, potato starch, and cocoa powder and set aside. Place a damp kitchen towel under the bowl to prevent it from sliding.

• Measure the milk mixture ingredients into a 2-quart, heavy-bottomed saucepan and set aside.

• Measure the flavorings into two separate bowls and set aside.

2. Bring the milk mixture to a boil over medium-high heat.

3. Once it reaches a boil, slowly pour the milk mixture into the yolk mixture, whisking slowly in small circles at first and ending with broader strokes until fully combined. Pour the mixture back into the saucepan.

4. Return the saucepan to the stove and heat over medium heat, whisking constantly but not rapidly, for about 4 minutes (3 minutes at high altitude). The key is to keep the pastry cream moving so it won't scorch on the bottom of the saucepan.

5. When you begin to see lava bubbles—large, slowly forming bubbles that burp steam—reduce the heat to the lowest setting and whisk briskly for 1 minute to pasteurize the pastry cream.

6. Pour the pastry cream into the bowl of a standing mixer fitted with the wire whip attachment. Whip the pastry cream on high speed until it's cooled to room temperature, about 4 to 5 minutes.

7. Reduce the mixer speed to medium-low and add the butter 1 tablespoon at a time, followed by the cocoa nibs and vanilla extract. Whip on medium speed until smooth, about 3 minutes.

Flame

This recipe is a study in pepper. I love the cayenne pepper in Sassy (page 40), so I decided to try a buttercream built around ancho chile peppers. I wanted to explore the flavor of the chile without the searing heat. I didn't want a buttercream that acts as a hot sauce and tries to burn you alive—Flame will not make you call for the fire brigade. Cake is all about pleasure, so kick back and enjoy this frosting on cupcakes or give some unsuspecting guests a pleasant surprise.

I thought of this recipe while on a jog in Rock Creek Park in Washington, DC. I had a specific role in mind for the four major elements: salt, sugar, cinnamon, and cocoa butter. The salt merely whets the palate, preparing it for the minor pepper burn that's just around the bend. The sugar blocks and covers the majority of the pepper's heat in its sprint to the taste buds. The cinnamon lends sweetness without sugar to every nook and cranny of the palate. The cocoa butter creates a cooling sensation as it melts away, absorbing heat from your mouth. I went a little overboard with the flavor theory on this one, but it was a long run and I had time to ponder.

EQUIPMENT: mixing bowls, standing mixer, 2-quart, heavy-bottomed saucepan, fine-mesh sieve

YIELD: 4 to 5 cups (enough for one 9-inch-round, three-layer cake or 24 cupcakes)

INGREDIENTS

Milk Mixture

vanilla bean, 1

dried ancho chile pepper, 1

whole milk, 1 cup

extra-fine granulated sugar,
2 ounces (¼ cup)

ground cayenne pepper, ½ teaspoon

unsalted butter, at room temperature,
2 ounces (½ stick)

Yolk Mixture

yolks (large), 6

extra-fine granulated sugar, 8 ounces (1 cup)

potato starch, 2 tablespoons

salt, ¼ teaspoon

ground cinnamon, ¼ teaspoon

Flavorings and Butter

cocoa butter, solid, ¼ cup

confectioners' sugar, ¼ cup (1 ounce)

paprika, ½ teaspoon

vanilla extract, 1 teaspoon

unsalted butter, at room temperature,
1 pound (4 sticks)

Sprinkling Mixture

turbinado sugar, 2 tablespoons

kosher salt, ¼ teaspoon

1. Set out the ingredients and equipment.

• Slice the vanilla bean lengthwise with a paring knife and scrape out the seeds. Reserve the pod for another use.

• Slice open the pepper and discard the seeds. Break the pepper into small pieces.

• Measure the other milk mixture ingredients into a 2-quart, heavy-bottomed saucepan. Add the vanilla bean seeds and chile pepper, stir to combine, and bring to a simmer over medium-high heat. Turn off the heat and let the mixture steep for 30 minutes.

• Separate the yolks into a large bowl. Add the 8 ounces sugar, the potato starch, salt, and cinnamon and whisk to combine. Place a damp kitchen towel under the bowl to prevent it from sliding.

• Measure the cocoa butter into a bowl and set aside.

• Sift the confectioners' sugar into a bowl on a scale for accurate measuring.

• Measure the vanilla extract and paprika into separate bowls and set aside.

• Measure the turbinado sugar and kosher salt into a small bowl and combine with your fingers.

2. Pour the steeped milk mixture into the bowl of a food processor and puree it into a paste—it will be very thick.

3. Return the puree to the saucepan and bring to a simmer over medium heat. Once it reaches a simmer, slowly pour it into the yolk mixture, whisking slowly in small circles at first and ending with broader strokes until fully combined. Add 2 ounces of butter, but do not stir in. Pour the mixture back into the saucepan.

4. Return the saucepan to the stove and heat over medium heat, whisking constantly but not rapidly, for about 4 minutes (3 minutes at high altitude). The key is to keep the pastry cream moving so it won't scorch on the bottom of the saucepan.

5. When you begin to see lava bubbles—large, slowly forming bubbles that burp steam—reduce the heat to the lowest setting and whisk briskly for 1 minute to pasteurize the pastry cream.

6. Pour the pastry cream into the bowl of a standing mixer fitted with the wire whip attachment. Add the cocoa butter. Whip the pastry cream on high speed until it's cooled to room temperature, about 4 to 5 minutes.

7. Reduce the mixer speed to low and add the confectioners' sugar, paprika, vanilla extract, and the butter 1 tablespoon at a time. Whip on medium speed until smooth, 2 to 3 minutes.

8. Frost a cake or cupcakes with the buttercream. As an option, lightly sprinkle tiny pinches of the sugar-salt mixture on top of the frosted cake.

Coconut Buttercream

This is the creamiest, dreamiest, most sensational buttercream I've ever made—it was the first I'd ever created. I remember sheepishly bringing the frosted cake into work and placing it in the kitchen without a note to take credit, then making a beeline back to my desk. Its debut got a great reception and it continues to be one of my favorites at CakeLove. We pair it with chocolate cake and call it NGC—New German Chocolate. Once a whole cake was returned without a single slice taken because it didn't look like a regular German Chocolate Cake. But that's why I like it.

This is a pastry cream–based buttercream that relies on coconut steeped in milk to deliver rich undertones. Dark brown sugar can be used, but muscovado is worth buying for the special accents it lends.

EQUIPMENT: mixing bowls, 2-quart, heavy-bottomed saucepan, standing mixer

YIELD: 4 to 5 cups (enough for two 9-inch-round, three-layer cakes or 24 cupcakes)

INGREDIENTS

Milk Mixture

whole milk, 2 cups

unsweetened coconut flakes,
   3 ounces (½ cup)

extra-fine granulated sugar, 7 ounces
   (¾ cup + 2 tablespoons)

Yolk Mixture

yolks (large), 6

extra-fine granulated sugar, 2 ounces (¼ cup)

potato starch, 3 tablespoons

unsalted butter, at room temperature,
   2 ounces (½ stick)

Flavorings and Butter

muscovado or dark brown sugar, 3 ounces
   (¼ cup), packed

coconut rum, 1 tablespoon

vanilla extract, 2 teaspoons

unsalted butter, chilled, 1 pound (4 sticks)

Chocolate Butter Cake with Coconut Buttercream

1. Set out the ingredients and equipment.

• Separate the yolks into a large bowl. Add the 2 ounces sugar and the potato starch and whisk to combine. Add the 2 ounces butter, but do not stir in. Place a damp kitchen towel under the bowl to prevent it from sliding.

• Measure the milk mixture ingredients into a 2-quart, heavy-bottomed saucepan and bring to a boil over medium-high heat. Turn off the heat and let the mixture steep for 10 minutes.

• Measure the flavorings into three separate bowls and set aside.

2. Return the milk mixture to a simmer. Once it reaches a simmer, slowly pour it into the yolk mixture, whisking slowly in small circles at first and ending with broader strokes until fully combined. Pour the mixture back into the saucepan.

3. Return the saucepan to the stove and heat over medium heat, whisking constantly but not rapidly, for about 4 minutes (3 minutes at high altitude). The key is to keep the pastry cream moving so it won't scorch on the bottom of the saucepan.

4. When you begin to see lava bubbles—large, slowly forming bubbles that burp steam—reduce the heat to the lowest setting and whisk briskly for 1 minute to pasteurize the pastry cream.

5. Pour the pastry cream into the bowl of a standing mixer fitted with the wire whip attachment. Add the muscovado, coconut rum, and vanilla extract. Whip the pastry cream on high speed until it's cooled to room temperature, about 4 to 5 minutes.

6. Reduce the mixer speed to medium-low and add the pound of butter, 1 tablespoon at a time. Whip on medium speed until smooth, about 2 to 3 minutes.

Cues

In college I grew to love summer squash. It's cheap, keeps for a long time, and absorbs flavor—perfect for the college-budget diet! I especially like zucchini. It has a great texture that bursts with its own juices when it's served hot. There were a lot of distractions around when I cooked in my college dorm, so I didn't hover over the stove. Sautéing the zucchini to the right point was impossible until I recognized an easy clue. I relied on what I heard, not what I saw or smelled. As the zucchini approached the threshold between being succulent or being limp, the rate at which water bubbles popped in the sauté pan slowed down—when the popping slowed the zukes were ready.

Using alternative cues worked then and it still works now. Italian meringue thickens as it cools, which is evident in the subtle change in the sound of the whip revolving in the bowl. There's a deeper thump with each pass of the wire whip. Always keep your senses alert when working in the kitchen. It can help you notice when something is amiss or, better yet, when everything is right and the dish is ready for the next move.

Hazelnut Crunch Buttercream

> *It's like ice cream and candy smashed together.*

Following the process for Coconut Buttercream, I created this recipe thinking that any nut steeped in milk should release its flavorful oils right into the liquid. The infusion of flavors works beautifully with hazelnuts.

This recipe calls for a lot of hazelnuts. They're roasted after steeping, which gives the buttercream a lot of crunch in every bite. It's more like chunky ice cream instead of plain old frosting. I use blanched hazelnuts to make the preparation easier. The alternative is using raw hazelnuts, which require roasting and rubbing in a towel to release the skins prior to use. This is cumbersome and time consuming, and I prefer to avoid this step.

Hazelnut-Crunch Buttercream works well with Chocolate Butter Cake (page 97) or Yellow Butter Cake (page 99), but I prefer it with the yellow cake because the flavors complement one another very nicely. It's also great paired with Maple Pound Cake (page 89). No matter what type of cake this buttercream is paired with, spread it on thick between cake layers and, since this is a heavier buttercream, leave the sides exposed.

EQUIPMENT: mixing bowls, 2-quart, heavy-bottomed saucepan, fine-mesh sieve, standing mixer

YIELD: 4 to 5 cups (enough for two 9-inch-round, three-layer cakes or 24 cupcakes)

INGREDIENTS

Yolk Mixture

yolks (large), 6

extra-fine granulated sugar, 2 ounces (¼ cup)

potato starch, 3 tablespoons

unsalted butter (at room temperature), 2 ounces (½ stick)

Milk Mixture

whole milk, 2 cups

unsalted hazelnuts, blanched and peeled, 3 ounces (⅔ cup)

extra-fine granulated sugar, 7 ounces (¾ cup + 2 tablespoons)

Flavorings and Butter

muscovado or dark brown sugar, 3 ounces (¼ cup), packed

hazelnut liqueur, 1 tablespoon

vanilla extract, 2 teaspoons

unsalted butter, at room temperature, 1 pound (4 sticks)

extra-fine granulated sugar, 2 ounces (¼ cup)

1. Preheat the oven to 350°F (conventional) or 335°F (convection).

2. Set out the ingredients and equipment.

• Separate the yolks into a large bowl. Add the 2 ounces sugar and the potato starch, whisk to combine and set aside. Add the 2 ounces butter but do not stir in. Place a damp kitchen towel under the bowl to prevent it from sliding.

• Measure the milk mixture ingredients into a 2-quart, heavy-bottomed saucepan and bring to a boil over medium-high heat. Turn off the heat and let the mixture steep for 10 minutes.

• Measure the flavorings into three separate bowls and set aside.

3. Strain the hazelnuts in a fine-mesh sieve over a large bowl to capture the flavored milk. Leave the nuts in the sieve to drain over a medium-sized bowl—you'll use them later.

4. Return the steeped milk to the saucepan and bring to a simmer over medium heat. Slowly pour it into the yolk mixture, whisking slowly in small circles at first and ending with broader strokes until fully combined. Pour the mixture back into the saucepan.

5. Return the saucepan to the stove and heat over medium heat, whisking constantly but not rapidly, for about 4 minutes (3 minutes at high altitude). The key is to keep the pastry cream moving so it won't scorch on the bottom of the saucepan.

6. When you begin to see lava bubbles—large, slowly forming bubbles that burp steam—reduce the heat to the lowest setting and whisk briskly for 1 minute to pasteurize the pastry cream.

7. Pour the pastry cream into the bowl of a standing mixer fitted with the wire whip attachment. Add the muscovado, hazelnut liqueur, and vanilla extract. Whip the pastry cream on high speed until it's cooled to room temperature, about 4 to 5 minutes.

8. Reduce the mixer speed to medium-low and add the butter 1 tablespoon at a time. Whip on medium speed until smooth, 2 to 3 minutes.

9. Meanwhile, toss the drained hazelnuts with ¼ cup sugar in a medium-sized bowl. Place on an ungreased parchment–lined sheet pan. Toast for 5 to 10 minutes (about 15 minutes for high altitude). Keep a close eye on the nuts—they tend to burn quickly.

10. Let the hazelnuts cool thoroughly before breaking them into chunks. Fold them into the buttercream—or mix on low speed—until the nuts are fully incorporated.

When the Milk Jumps

I learned the hard way when making pastry cream and ganache. When you're heating milk or cream in a saucepan, remove it from the heat once it begins to simmer, or watch it closely. The temperature goes through a series of plateaus, and once milk or cream reaches a simmer, it can quickly boil over.

Ingredients

Steep the nuts

Whisk in starch and sugar

Whisk milk into yolk mixture

Whisk over medium heat until lava bubbles appear

Whip on high until cool, add butter

Break apart toasted nuts

Fold nuts into buttercream

Pecan Crunch Buttercream

Pecans always make me think of the holidays. When I was young, my family would visit Ted and Elaine Long and their daughters to enjoy the long winter nights by their roaring fire and beautiful Christmas tree. Mrs. Long is from Louisiana and always has pecans around for cracking.

This buttercream is about as outrageous and decadent as it gets! It's closer to butter pecan ice cream than buttercream. I developed this as a delightful partner for the Maple Pound Cake (page 89) and the combination is captivating.

Equipment: mixing bowls, 2-quart, heavy-bottomed saucepan, fine-mesh sieve, standing mixer

Yield: 4 to 5 cups (enough for two 9-inch-round, three-layer cakes or 24 cupcakes)

INGREDIENTS

Yolk Mixture

yolks (large), 6

extra-fine granulated sugar, 2 ounces (¼ cup)

potato starch, 3 tablespoons

unsalted butter, at room temperature,
   2 ounces (½ stick)

Milk Mixture

whole milk, 2 cups

unsalted pecans, halved, 3 ounces
   (1 cup)

extra-fine granulated sugar, 7 ounces
   (¾ cup + 2 tablespoons)

Flavorings and Butter

muscovado or dark brown sugar, 3 ounces
   (¼ cup), packed

crystallized or raw honey, 1 tablespoon

vanilla extract, 2 teaspoons

unsalted butter, chilled, 1 pound (4 sticks)

extra-fine granulated sugar, 2 ounces (¼ cup)

1. Preheat the oven to 350°F (conventional) or 335°F (convection).

2. Set out the ingredients and equipment.

• Separate the yolks into a large bowl. Add the 2 ounces sugar and the potato starch, whisk to combine and set aside. Add the 2 ounces butter but do not stir in. Place a damp kitchen towel under the bowl to prevent it from sliding.

• Measure the milk mixture ingredients into a 2-quart, heavy-bottomed saucepan and bring to a boil over medium-high heat. Turn off the heat and let the mixture steep for 10 minutes.

• Measure the flavorings into three separate bowls and set aside.

3. Strain the pecans in a fine-mesh sieve over a large bowl to capture the flavored milk. Leave the nuts in the sieve to drain over a medium-sized bowl—you'll use them later.

4. Return the steeped milk to the saucepan and bring to a simmer over medium heat. Once it reaches a simmer, slowly pour it into the yolk mixture, whisking slowly in small circles at first and ending with broader strokes until fully combined. Pour the mixture back into the saucepan.

5. Return the saucepan to the stove and heat over medium heat, whisking constantly but not rapidly, for about 4 minutes (3 minutes at high altitude). The key is to keep the pastry cream moving so it won't scorch on the bottom of the saucepan.

6. When you begin to see lava bubbles—large, slowly forming bubbles that burp steam—reduce the heat to the lowest setting and whisk briskly for 1 minute to pasteurize the pastry cream.

7. Pour the pastry cream into the bowl of a standing mixer fitted with the wire whip attachment. Add the muscovado, honey, and vanilla extract. Whip the pastry cream on high speed until it's cooled to room temperature, about 4 to 5 minutes.

8. Reduce the mixer speed to medium-low and add the butter 1 tablespoon at a time. Whip on medium speed until smooth, 2 to 3 minutes.

9. Meanwhile, toss the drained pecans with ¼ cup sugar in a medium-sized bowl. Place on an ungreased parchment–lined sheet pan. Toast for 5 to 10 minutes (about 15 minutes for high altitude). Keep a close eye on the nuts—they tend to turn quickly from toasted to charred.

10. Let the pecans cool thoroughly before breaking them into chunks with your fingers. Add them to the buttercream and mix on low speed until the nuts are fully incorporated.

11. Spread the buttercream on thick between cake layers and leave the sides exposed.

Lava Bubbles

Lava bubbles is my term for the large bubbles that form when cooking a pastry cream or custard. The bubbles vent steam similar to the way molten lava burps steam. They are my visual cue that the cream or custard is nearly finished cooking. After the lava bubbles appear I turn the temperature all the way down and rapidly stir for 30 to 60 seconds to pasteurize it and guarantee that it's cooked. This is my alternative to the standard test of running a finger over the back of a wooden spoon coated with the custard and waiting to see if it comes together. If you've ever done that you know that the custard is blazing hot and can be painful to touch. Lava bubbles are a convenient (and painless) warning that scorching is imminent.

Peanut Crunch Buttercream

Even though peanuts are really legumes (beans), they behave a lot like nuts. In this buttercream, peanuts create a sensational flavor and rich texture. It's not overwhelming and it doesn't taste like chunky peanut butter—instead it's much more subtle. I like pairing this with Chocolate Butter Cake (page 97) or Chocolate Pound Cake (page 37).

Be sure to use unsalted peanuts. And if you buy raw or boiled peanuts, roast them until they're barely golden prior to steeping in the milk to achieve the right flavor.

EQUIPMENT: mixing bowls, 2-quart, heavy-bottomed saucepan, fine-mesh sieve, standing mixer

YIELD: 4 to 5 cups (enough for two 9-inch-round, three-layer cakes or 24 cupcakes)

INGREDIENTS

Yolk Mixture

yolks (large), 6

extra-fine granulated sugar, 2 ounces (¼ cup)

potato starch, 3 tablespoons

unsalted butter, at room temperature,
   2 ounces (½ stick)

Milk Mixture

whole milk, 2 cups

unsalted roasted peanuts, 3 ounces (½ cup)

extra-fine granulated sugar, 7 ounces (¾ cup
   + 2 tablespoons)

Flavorings and Butter

muscovado or dark brown sugar, 3 ounces
   (¼ cup), packed

crystallized or raw honey, 1 tablespoon

natural peanut butter, 1 tablespoon

vanilla extract, 2 teaspoons

unsalted butter, chilled, 1 pound (4 sticks)

extra-fine granulated sugar, ¼ cup

1. Preheat the oven to 350°F (conventional) or 335°F (convection).

2. Set out the ingredients and equipment.

• Separate the yolks into a large bowl. Add the 2 ounces sugar and the potato starch and set aside. Add the 2 ounces butter but do not stir in. Place a damp kitchen towel under the bowl to prevent it from sliding.

• Measure the milk mixture ingredients into a 2-quart, heavy-bottomed saucepan and bring to a boil over medium-high heat. Turn off the heat and let the mixture steep for 10 minutes.

• Measure the flavorings into three separate bowls and set aside.

3. Strain the peanuts in a fine-mesh sieve over a large bowl to capture the flavored milk. Leave the nuts in the sieve to drain over a medium-sized bowl—you'll use them later.

4. Return the steeped milk to the saucepan and bring to a simmer over medium heat. Once it reaches a simmer, slowly pour it into the yolk mixture, whisking slowly in small circles at first and ending with broader strokes until fully combined. Pour the mixture back into the saucepan.

5. Return the saucepan to the stove and heat over medium heat, whisking constantly but not rapidly, for about 4 minutes (3 minutes at high altitude). The key is to keep the pastry cream moving so it won't scorch on the bottom of the saucepan.

6. When you begin to see lava bubbles—large, slowly forming bubbles that burp steam—reduce the heat to the lowest setting and whisk briskly for 1 minute to pasteurize the pastry cream.

7. Pour the pastry cream into the bowl of a standing mixer fitted with the wire whip attachment. Add the muscovado, honey, peanut butter, and vanilla extract. Whip the pastry cream on high speed until it's cooled to room temperature, about 4 to 5 minutes.

8. Reduce the mixer speed to medium-low and add the butter 1 tablespoon at a time. Whip on medium speed until smooth, 2 to 3 minutes.

9. Meanwhile, toss the drained peanuts with ¼ cup sugar in a medium-sized bowl. Place on an ungreased parchment-lined sheet pan. Toast for 5 to 10 minutes (about 15 minutes for high altitude). Keep a close eye on the nuts—they tend to turn quickly from toasted to charred.

10. Let the peanuts cool thoroughly before breaking them into chunks with your fingers. Add them to the buttercream and mix on low speed until the nuts are fully incorporated.

11. Spread the buttercream on thick between cake layers and leave the sides exposed.

Seven-Minute Meringue Frosting

This classic frosting is easy enough to make without a recipe and comes together in just a few minutes. Use equal weights of egg whites and sugar, gently whisk them over simmering water until they're slightly warm to the touch, then whip on high with the standing mixer. Sometimes it takes seven minutes to get there, sometimes it doesn't. Either way, it's a fast preparation and tastes delicious.

This thick, dense cooked meringue can be spread on the cake of your choice. Be sure to spread it only on a cooled cake. A warm cake will not be firm enough and could be torn apart by spreading the meringue.

EQUIPMENT: standing mixer, 2-quart, heavy-bottomed saucepan

YIELD: 4 to 5 cups (enough for two 9-inch-round, three-layer cakes or 24 cupcakes)

INGREDIENTS
Meringue
extra-fine granulated sugar, 8 ounces (1 cup)
egg whites (large), 7

1. Find a saucepan that is large enough to accommodate the bowl from the standing mixer to create a double boiler. Add water to the saucepan, but keep the water level just below where the bottom of the bowl will rest. Bring the water to a simmer over medium-high heat.

2. Meanwhile, in the mixer bowl, gently whisk the egg whites and sugar to combine.

3. Set the mixer bowl over the simmering water, whisking the mixture constantly and slowly. The goal is to bring the mixture to body temperature (around 98°F) without curdling the egg whites.

4. Move the mixer bowl to the mixer fitted with the wire whip attachment and whip on high speed until the meringue is thick, glossy, and cool, about 5 minutes.

Whipped Cream

Whipped cream is essential for completing the Black Forest Cake (page 138), and it works for many others too. In order to avoid overbeating and ruining the cream—which is rather easy to do— I like to finish whipping it by hand with a whisk. Moving away from the mixer at the end and putting it in your own hands is an easy way to keep everything under control.

Basic Whipped Cream

This topping will work as an accompaniment to nearly any cake if you want to skip making a buttercream. It's never wrong to serve dessert with homemade whipped cream!

EQUIPMENT: standing mixer, whisk

YIELD: 2 to 4 cups

INGREDIENTS

heavy cream, 2 cups
confectioners' sugar, 2 tablespoons
vanilla extract, ½ teaspoon

1. Place the mixing bowl and wire whip attachment from a standing mixer in the freezer for 10 to 15 minutes to chill.
2. Sift the confectioners' sugar to remove any lumps.
3. Combine all of the ingredients in the chilled bowl and whip on medium to medium-high speed for 2 to 3 minutes, or until medium peaks form.
4. Remove the bowl and lightly whip by hand with a whisk to the desired stiffness.

Whipped Cream with Honey

Raw honey is unprocessed and naturally crystallized. Its flavor is much more dramatic and noticeable than regular clover honey. Regular honey is perfectly acceptable to use but if you can find raw honey in the baking aisle of your grocery store, try it. This pairs wonderfully with the Cinnamon and Cream Layer Cake (page 133).

EQUIPMENT: standing mixer, 2-quart, heavy-bottomed saucepan

YIELD: 4 to 5 cups (enough for two 9-inch-round, three-layer cakes or 24 cupcakes)

INGREDIENTS
Whipped Cream

heavy cream, 2½ cups
confectioners' sugar, ¼ cup
vanilla extract, 1 teaspoon
raw honey, 1 teaspoon

1. Place the mixing bowl and wire whip attachment from a standing mixer in the freezer for 10 to 15 minutes to chill.

2. Sift the confectioners' sugar to remove any lumps.

3. Combine all of the ingredients in the chilled bowl and whip on medium to medium-high speed for about 30 seconds, or until soft to medium peaks form.

Remove the bowl and lightly whip by hand with a whisk to the desired stiffness.

Whipped Cream with Cinnamon

Add a touch of spice to bring another layer of flavor to whatever you're serving with this unique whipped cream. You can also substitute a different spice if you like—allspice, nutmeg, clove, and mace all work well.

EQUIPMENT: standing mixer, 2-quart, heavy-bottomed saucepan

YIELD: 4 to 5 cups (enough for two 9-inch-round, three-layer cakes or 24 cupcakes)

INGREDIENTS
Whipped Cream
heavy cream, 2 cups
confectioners' sugar, 2 tablespoons
vanilla extract, ½ teaspoon
ground cinnamon, ⅛ teaspoon

1. Place the mixing bowl and wire whip attachment from a standing mixer in the freezer for 10 to 15 minutes to chill.

2. Sift the confectioners' sugar to remove any lumps.

3. Combine the heavy cream, confectioners' sugar, and vanilla extract in the chilled bowl and whip on medium to medium-high speed for about 30 seconds, or until soft to medium peaks form.

4. Remove the bowl. Add the cinnamon and lightly whip by hand with a whisk to the desired stiffness.

Ganache

Make heads turn and knees buckle with this incredibly simple finishing touch of chocolate blended with heavy cream.

Not all bittersweet chocolates have the same intensity. Some are bolder than others—it all depends on the percentage of chocolate mass. I prefer bittersweet chocolate with a 60% chocolate mass. Anything over 55% chocolate mass is considered bittersweet, and from what I've seen, even people who don't like chocolate enjoy bittersweet. It's unmistakably chocolate, but not over the edge. I'd say anything that's in the 66–72% range is for chocolate lovers only. Going higher than 72% is not recommended for ganache.

Needless to say, the manufacturing process matters, too. Look for brands that use only the best-quality ingredients.

EQUIPMENT: standing mixer, 2-quart, heavy-bottomed saucepan, mixing bowl, whisk

YIELD: 4 to 5 cups (enough for two 9-inch-round, three-layer cakes or 24 cupcakes)

INGREDIENTS
Ganache

60% bittersweet chocolate pistoles, 1½ cups

heavy cream, 1 cup

1. In a 2-quart, heavy-bottomed saucepan, bring the cream to a light simmer over medium heat.

2. Meanwhile, measure the chocolate and place it in a medium-sized, heat-resistant mixing bowl.

3. Once the cream reaches a light simmer, pour it over the chocolate. Wait about 10 seconds for the cream to work its way into all of the crevices between the pieces of chocolate, then whisk to combine.

4. Let the ganache cool for 5 to 10 minutes before using. If the ganache is too warm it will melt the crumb coat of buttercream and won't adhere to the cake's surface.

Chocolate Butter Cake with vanilla-flavored Italian Meringue Buttercream and Ganache

Glazing Chocolate

This thin version of ganache provides a dark, smooth glaze that races all the way down any Bundt, pound cake, or Crunchy Feet for a pleasing visual effect.

EQUIPMENT: 2-quart, heavy bottomed saucepan, mixing bowl

YIELD: about 3 cups (enough for one 12-cup Bundt cake or 24 Crunchy Feet

---

INGREDIENTS

Glaze

heavy cream, 1½ cups

vanilla extract, 2 teaspoons

60% bittersweet chocolate pistoles, 1 cup

1. Set the cooled cake on a wire rack with wax or parchment paper underneath it to catch any drips.

2. Combine the heavy cream and vanilla extract in a saucepan and bring to a simmer over medium heat, stirring constantly.

3. Meanwhile, place the chocolate in a medium-sized nonreactive mixing bowl, preferably one with a handle and a small pouring spout.

4. Remove the hot vanilla-cream mixture from the heat and pour over the chocolate. Let the heat from the cream melt the chocolate for 10 to 20 seconds, then gently whisk until smooth.

5. Immediately pour the glaze over the cake. For a Bundt cake, pour the glaze in a thin, steady stream in a crisscross fashion, working your way around the cake for even coverage. If you want more chocolate on the cake, repeat until it looks right. This is a rich glaze, so let restraint be your guide. For Crunchy Feet, pour about 2 tablespoons of glaze directly onto the top of each one, letting it drizzle down the sides.

6. If the bowl is empty before you're finished glazing, scrape any chocolate that has drizzled onto the parchment and reuse it for the remaining Crunchy Feet.

7. Serve immediately, while the glaze is still warm.

Chocolate Pound Cake with Ganache and melted white chocolate

Melting Chocolate

Never melt or warm chocolate or ganache over direct heat. It's fragile and has a low melting point, about 88°F. I learned this the hard way. The first time I melted chocolate I had it in a saucepan directly on the burner—what a mistake! Now I use the double-boiler method. To do this, place a heat-resistant (stainless steel) bowl of chocolate over steaming, never boiling, water. Never let the bottom of the bowl touch the water or the chocolate may scorch. Occasionally stir the chocolate to distribute the heat evenly. Remove from the heat when the chocolate is melted and has a smooth glossy appearance. Allow it to cool for 5 to 10 minutes before using. Microwaving works well, too, though I don't use a microwave when I bake. If you use a microwave, heat the chocolate in short intervals and stir it often.

Fruit Glazes

Putting a glaze on a cake elevates it to something irresistible. It makes the presentation extra special and even helps to preserve the freshness of the cake. All of the fruit preserve glazes here require the basic steps of straining heated fruit preserves through a metal strainer and brushing on the glaze. The trick is in the final step, when the glaze-covered cake gets a quick blast in the oven to set its new, glistening exterior. It's an easy move that makes a simple Bundt or pound cake look really impressive. Heating the preserves over low heat prepares them for straining. Using medium heat is OK but watch the saucepan closely—preserves have a lot of sugar and will burn easily. If the preserves scorch, the flavor is ruined and they are no longer usable for the glaze.

Apricot Preserve

This is the standard fruit preserve glaze for a Bundt cake. It works well because of the neutral color and mild sweet flavor of the strained preserves. I happen to love apricot preserves but if you'd prefer not to use them, try peach preserves instead. They'll work just as well.

If you're not OK with using alcohol, substitute water for the rum or omit it altogether.

EQUIPMENT: 2-quart, heavy-bottomed saucepan, fine-mesh sieve, mixing bowls, pastry brush

YIELD: about ⅓ cup (enough for one 12-cup Bundt cake)

INGREDIENTS

Glaze

apricot preserves, ½ cup

confectioners' sugar, 3 tablespoons

cold water, 1 tablespoon

rum (optional), 1 teaspoon

Lemon

This glaze pairs nicely with citrus pound cakes, especially if you want to amplify the fresh, citrus flavor.

EQUIPMENT: 2-quart, heavy-bottomed saucepan, fine-mesh sieve, mixing bowls, pastry brush

YIELD: about ⅓ cup (enough for one 12-cup Bundt cake)

INGREDIENTS

Glaze

orange marmalade, ½ cup

confectioners' sugar, 6 tablespoons

lemon juice, 3 tablespoons

vanilla extract, 1 teaspoon

Cherry Preserve

This glaze is perfect for any of the chocolate pound cakes.

EQUIPMENT: 2-quart, heavy-bottomed saucepan, fine-mesh sieve, mixing bowls, pastry brush

YIELD: about ⅓ cup (enough for one 12-cup Bundt cake)

INGREDIENTS
Glaze
cherry preserves, ½ cup

confectioners' sugar, 3 tablespoons

dark rum, 1 tablespoon

Spiced

Try this glaze to add an exciting dimension to the Mojito Pound Cake (page 65) or any other cake with cinnamon, clove, nutmeg, mace, or allspice.

EQUIPMENT: 2-quart, heavy-bottomed saucepan, fine-mesh sieve, mixing bowls, pastry brush

YIELD: about ⅓ cup (enough for one 12-cup Bundt cake)

INGREDIENTS
Glaze
peach preserves, ½ cup

confectioners' sugar, 3 tablespoons

dark rum, 1 tablespoon

ground cloves, ½ teaspoon

ground allspice, pinch

1. Preheat the oven to 350°F (conventional) or 335°F (convection).

2. Place the cake on an oven-safe plate.

3. Heat the preserves in a saucepan over low heat until the preserves liquefy, about 3 to 4 minutes.

4. Transfer the heated preserves to a sieve placed over a bowl and press with a rubber spatula to separate the liquid from the solids.

5. Brush a light coat of the warm preserve liquid onto the cake with a pastry brush.

6. Combine the remaining ingredients in a small bowl and lightly brush the mixture onto the preserve-coated cake.

7. Bake for 5 minutes to seal in the glaze.

8. Remove the cake from the oven and let it cool to room temperature before serving.

Fillings

Inside every cake should be a fantastic filling.

The first recipe I ever made was a barbeque sauce when I was eleven. Since then I've always had a thing for sauces, and a pastry cream is basically a sauce that's stabilized through cooking and the use of a touch of flour.

Pastry creams are often the featured story in the middle of the cake—the part that oozes out when your fork cuts through a slice for another bite. I especially like the contrast of temperatures when eating a cake filled with any kind of custard. Nothing beats simplicity when it comes to cake fillings.

At CakeLove, vanilla, chocolate, and lemon are the top three flavors. All of these fillings will keep in the fridge for up to 7 days. These fillings—and the meringues in the next chapter—will work well for many of the cakes, especially the basics: chocolate and vanilla. I encourage you to mix and match the components as you see fit; when you're baking from scratch, the flavors will blend nicely in almost any combination. But don't get carried away when creating your dream cake—a cake never needs more than three flavors in play.

Vanilla Pastry Cream

No book on cakes would be complete without a vanilla pastry cream recipe. This delicious concoction comes straight from CakeLove and wins many compliments. When placed between layers of cake it soaks in just enough to moisten them without making them soggy. I love the vanilla pastry cream sandwiched between three layers of vanilla cake smothered in chocolate ganache—it's our Boston Cream Downfall.

EQUIPMENT: 2-quart, heavy-bottomed saucepan, mixing bowls

YIELD: 1 quart (enough for one 9-inch-round, three-layer cake)

INGREDIENTS

Milk Mixture

whole milk, 2½ cups
vanilla bean, 1

Yolk Mixture

yolks (large), 6
vanilla extract, 1 teaspoon
extra-fine granulated sugar, 5½ ounces
(½ cup + 3 tablespoons)
unbleached all-purpose flour
1½ ounces (5 tablespoons)

1. Set out the ingredients and equipment.

• Measure the milk into a 2-quart, heavy-bottomed saucepan.

• Slice the vanilla bean lengthwise with a paring knife and scrape out the seeds. Add the seeds and the pod to the milk, stir to combine, and bring to a boil over medium heat. Turn off the heat and let the mixture steep for 10 minutes.

• Separate the yolks into a large bowl, add the vanilla extract, sugar, and flour, and whisk to combine. Set aside.

2. Return the milk mixture to a simmer. Once it reaches a simmer, carefully remove the pod and discard. Slowly pour the milk into the yolk mixture, whisking slowly in small circles at first and ending with broader strokes until fully combined. Pour the mixture back into the saucepan.

3. Return the saucepan to the stove and heat over medium heat, whisking constantly but not rapidly, for about 4 minutes (3 minutes at high altitude). Keep the pastry cream moving so it won't scorch on the bottom of the saucepan.

4. When you begin to see lava bubbles—large, slowly forming bubbles that burp steam—reduce the heat to the lowest setting and whisk briskly for 1 minute to pasteurize the pastry cream.

5. Pour the pastry cream into a shallow, nonreactive mixing bowl, preferably stainless steel. Cover with plastic pressed against the surface of the pastry cream to prevent a skin from forming.

6. Immediately refrigerate the pastry cream for at least 3 hours. If you want to cool the pastry cream more rapidly, place the heat-resistant bowl of pastry cream over an ice bath and refrigerate both together.

Chocolate
Pastry
Cream

This pastry cream is for those who are obsessed with chocolate and like desserts on the sweeter side. I developed it before opening CakeLove, back when I was baking alone and could experiment on a daily basis. I wanted it to be thick, dark, messy, and arresting. Once it's cool enough, dip your finger and take a lick—this pastry cream is delicious right from the pot! The ingredients are a bit out of proportion in this recipe—it calls for a lot of sugar. The sugar helps insulate the cocoa powder from the burning while the pastry cream cooks. Some of the pastry cream will stick to the bottom of the pot during cooking, but that's necessary to get the final result. It all comes together at the last minute when the pastry cream begins to bubble with large, steam venting bubbles—what I call "lava bubbles"—and the color changes from a medium brown to a rich, dark brown.

EQUIPMENT: 2-quart, heavy-bottomed saucepan, mixing bowls

YIELD: 1 quart (enough for one 9-inch-round, three-layer cake)

INGREDIENTS
Milk

whole milk, 2 cups

Yolk Mixture

eggs (large), 3
yolks (large), 7
vanilla extract, 2 teaspoons

Dry Ingredients

extra-fine granulated sugar, 24 ounces
   (3 cups)
unsweetened cocoa powder, 2 ounces (½ cup)
potato starch, ¼ cup
unbleached all-purpose flour, 2 tablespoons

Butter

unsalted butter, chilled, 8 tablespoons
   (1 stick)

1. Set out the ingredients and equipment.

• Measure the milk into a 2-quart, heavy-bottomed saucepan.

• Crack the eggs and yolks into a separate bowl, add the vanilla extract, whisk to combine, and set aside. Place a damp towel underneath the bowl to prevent slippage.

• Measure the dry ingredients into a separate bowl and whisk for 10 seconds to blend. Set aside.

2. Bring the milk to a boil over medium heat. Remove from the heat, but keep the saucepan on the stove.

3. Whisk the yolk mixture into the dry ingredient mixture. It will be very thick so it'll take some effort.

4. Return the milk mixture to a simmer. Once it reaches a simmer, slowly pour it into the yolk mixture, whisking slowly in small circles at first and ending with broader strokes until fully combined. Pour the mixture back into the saucepan.

5. Return the saucepan to the stove and heat over medium heat, whisking constantly but not rapidly, for about 4 minutes (3 minutes at high altitude). The key is to keep the pastry cream moving so it won't scorch on the bottom of the saucepan.

6. When you begin to see lava bubbles—large, slowly forming bubbles that burp steam—reduce the heat to the lowest setting and whisk briskly for 1 minute to pasteurize the pastry cream.

7. Pour the pastry cream into a shallow, nonreactive mixing bowl, preferably stainless steel. Whisk in the butter 1 tablespoon at a time. Cover with plastic pressed against the surface of the pastry cream to prevent a skin from forming.

8. Immediately refrigerate the pastry cream for at least 3 hours. If you want to cool the pastry cream more rapidly, place the heat-resistant bowl of pastry cream over an ice bath and refrigerate both together.

Chocolate Butter Cake with Chocolate Pastry Cream, Chocolate Buttercream, and Ganache

Lemon
Curd

This is one of the simplest recipes for a wonderful jolt of lemon, perfect for filling layers of cake. With a naturally bright lemon flavor and a rich yellow color, it goes great with Yellow Butter Cake and lemon-flavored Italian Meringue Buttercream. The key to a successful curd is to keep the mixture moving steadily—the whisk is the easiest tool for this. You don't have to whip in air, just keep the ingredients moving in the saucepan. If you stop, the egg proteins will have a chance to curdle, which would ruin the texture of the curd. You can always remove any solids by passing the curd through a fine-mesh sieve or tamis, but straining the solids might not mask the error, as the cooked egg proteins may change the taste of the final product.

Rolling the lemons on the counter while pressing down firmly with the heel of your hand will release the juice and make squeezing the lemons easier.

EQUIPMENT: 2-quart, heavy bottomed saucepan, mixing bowls, fine-mesh sieve

YIELD: 2 cups (enough for one 9-inch-round three-layer cake)

INGREDIENTS
Filling

lemons, 4 to 5

extra-fine granulated sugar, 18 ounces
  (2¼ cups)

cornstarch, 2 teaspoons

eggs (large), 4

yolks (large), 4

unsalted butter, chilled, 6 ounces (1½ sticks)

Ingredients

1. Set out the required ingredients and equipment.

• Squeeze the lemons to make 1 cup of juice. Strain out the seeds. Set the juice aside.

• Measure the sugar and cornstarch into a 2-quart, heavy-bottomed saucepan, whisk to combine, and set aside.

• Crack the eggs and yolks into a separate bowl and set aside.

2. Whisk the lemon juice into the sugar mixture, followed by the eggs and yolks.

3. Whisk in the cold butter 1 tablespoon at a time.

4. Set the saucepan over medium heat and bring to a simmer, whisking continuously.

5. When you begin to see lava bubbles—large, slowly forming bubbles that burp steam—reduce the heat to the lowest setting and whisk briskly for 1 minute to pasteurize the lemon curd. (Lava bubbles usually appear in about 10 minutes—7 to 8 minutes for high altitude.)

6. If you wish to strain the lemon curd, pour it through a fine-mesh sieve into a nonreactive bowl, preferably stainless steel. If you're not straining the curd, pour it directly into a nonreactive mixing bowl. Cover with plastic pressed against the surface of the lemon curd to prevent a skin from forming.

7. Immediately refrigerate the lemon curd for at least 3 hours. If you want to cool the lemon curd more rapidly, place the heat-resistant bowl of lemon curd over an ice bath and refrigerate both together.

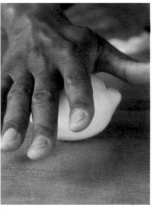
Roll the lemon

Juice the lemon

Add the lemon juice to the sugar

Add the eggs

Add the butter

Lemon curd at lava bubbles stage

Meringues

Lightly baked meringues are an elegant and dramatic way to dress up any cake.

Fully baked, dried-out meringues are a big no-no for me. They're way too sweet, they cut up the roof of my mouth, and they make a mess when eaten. I want meringues that are crisp and soft. Something that looks fluffy shouldn't tear up my lips and tongue, leaving me hoarse with a sugar burn.

In order to avoid meringue-inflicted wounds, I bake my meringues a little differently than most people. I follow the French tradition by adding a touch of flour, but the baking temperature veers into uncharted territory. I borrowed a method used in roasting turkey—blasting it with high heat to seal the outside. I know that sounds crazy but when I taught myself how to bake I borrowed ideas from wherever I could. I bake the meringues quickly at 335°F instead of at a low and slow 200°F for 2 to 3 hours. The high temperature makes a crisp shell that gives way to a soft, gooey, light center. They're delicate and delicious.

I like to pair meringues with a layer cake when I want to casually dress it up. And I know my guests will enjoy plucking them off the cake and popping them in their mouth as a dessert appetizer!

Keep the following pointers in mind when preparing the meringue recipes, each of which follows the same basic procedure.

• It is extremely important that your bowl and whisk attachment are completely clean and dry. Check your equipment and ingredients for all forms of fat, whether it's butter, oil, or yolks. Be especially watchful for bits of yolk that spill into the egg whites when separated. Any traces of fat will prevent the egg whites from whipping.

• Sift the confectioners' sugar to remove any lumps.

• It's not necessary to sift the flour for meringues because each recipe calls for only 2 tablespoons. If you need to make a gluten-free version, use potato starch instead but reduce the amount called for by half.

• In general, high altitude adjustments call for using three-quarters of the usual amount of sugar and baking twice as long as at sea level.

Ingredients

Whip the egg whites for stiff peak; add sugar

• Only fill the pastry bag halfway with meringue batter. An overloaded pastry bag is difficult and messy to close. Usually the bag will have to be filled two or three times.

• Be sure that all of the bulky ingredients—like chunks of chocolate—added to the batter will fit through the tip of the piping bag. A good rule of thumb is to break down any bulky items such as dried fruit or chocolate into ¼-inch pieces.

• You can use your creativity when piping these meringues. I prefer to make teardrops or swirls, but you could make S curves, lines, loops, right angles—the choice is yours! I pipe without a decorative tip on the bag because it's one less item to clean up, and I like the rounded look of the finished meringues. Also, sharp edges are usually lost on these batters because of the bulk or fat in the ingredients.

• Do not refrigerate meringues. Refrigeration deteriorates them and ruins all of your hard work.

Chocolate and Hazelnut Meringues dipped in Ganache

Sprinkle on the dry ingredients in 3 additions

Fold in the dry ingredienrts

Fill a pastry bag

Pipe out the meringues

Vanilla Meringues

This is my base recipe for meringues. I've created a lot of variations using this recipe as my starting point, and you too can add ingredients to this recipe to create new recipes, but remember to keep the size of the ingredients on the smaller side and don't use anything with a lot of water in it. Vanilla powder is available in the baking aisle of most grocery stores and by mail order (see Resources, page 218). It's not mandatory, so if it's unavailable just skip it.

EQUIPMENT: standing mixer, 15-inch pastry piping bag

YIELD: twenty to thirty 1-inch meringues or twelve to fifteen 2-inch meringues

---

INGREDIENTS

Meringue

egg whites (large), 4

extra-fine granulated sugar, 6 ounces
(¾ cup), *or 4½ ounces (½ cup + 1 table-spoon) at high altitude*

vanilla extract, ¼ teaspoon

Dry Ingredients

confectioners' sugar, 3 ounces (¾ cup)

unbleached all-purpose flour, 1 ounce +
2 tablespoons (5 tablespoons)

vanilla powder, 1 tablespoon

1. Preheat the oven to 335°F (conventional) or 325°F (convection). Set the rack in the middle of the oven.

2. Line a sheet pan with parchment or a nonstick silicone baking mat.

3. Set out the ingredients.

• Measure the meringue ingredients into three separate bowls and set aside.

• Measure the dry ingredients into a separate bowl and whisk for 10 seconds to blend. Set aside.

4. In the bowl of a standing mixer fitted with the wire whip attachment, whip the egg whites on high speed until stiff peaks form, 1 to 2 minutes.

5. With the mixer still on high speed, slowly add the sugar and whip for 15 seconds to incorporate. Add the vanilla extract and reduce the mixer speed to medium for about 15 seconds to stabilize the meringue.

6. Stop the mixer and remove the bowl. Tap the wire whip on the side of the mixer bowl to remove all the meringue. Fold the dry ingredients into the meringue in 3 additions using a rubber spatula, working gently to avoid deflating the meringue.

7. Holding a pastry bag in one hand at the halfway mark, fold the top half of the bag down to cover your hand. If it's a reusable bag fitted with a piping tip, insert the tip into the bag to prevent the meringue from dripping out when loading the batter. Scoop the meringue into the bag with the rubber spatula. If you're using a disposable bag, cut the tip off to make a hole about ½ inch in diameter.

8. Pipe the meringues onto the lined sheet pan about 1 inch apart to allow for spreading, which is usually minimal.

9. Follow the appropriate bake times listed below.

ITEM (EITHER RECIPE)	SEA LEVEL	HIGH ALTITUDE
1-inch meringues	7–9 minutes	10–12 minutes
2-inch meringues	14 minutes	20 minutes

10. The meringues are done when they appear dry and slightly browned.

11. Remove the pan from the oven and cool to room temperature, about 10 minutes on a flat, heat-resistant surface or a wire rack.

12. Once the meringues are cooled, gently slide an offset metal spatula under each one to release from the parchment. Enjoy them right away, use them to decorate a cake, or store in an airtight container at room temperature for up to 3 days.

Meringue Shapes

PIPING A TEARDROP

Hold the pastry bag about ½ inch above the lined sheet pan and gently squeeze out a dollop that's about 1 inch in diameter. Hold the bag steady and release pressure when the batter meets the tip. Stop applying pressure and gently lift the pastry bag straight up to create the meringue's peak.

PIPING A SWIRL

Hold the pastry bag about ½ inch above the lined sheet pan and gently squeeze out 2 to 3 tablespoons of meringue while slowly moving the bag in a clockwise motion for 2 revolutions. Raise the bag slowly as you pipe, trying to avoid creating gaps between the curves. Stop applying pressure and gently lift the pastry bag straight up to create the meringue's peak.

Chocolate Meringues

The crunchy crust on these meringues conceals a soft, creamy, gooey center. These are a perfect topper for any chocolate cake. To double up on the chocolate, let the baked meringues cool, then dip them in ganache.

EQUIPMENT: standing mixer, 15-inch pastry bag

YIELD: twenty to thirty 1-inch meringues or twelve to fifteen 2-inch meringues

---

INGREDIENTS

Meringue

egg whites (large), 4

extra-fine granulated sugar, 6 ounces
 (¾ cup), or 4½ ounces

Dry

confectioners' sugar, 3 ounces (¾ cup)

cocoa powder, 1 ounce

unbleached all-purpose flour, 2 tablespoons

1. Preheat the oven to 335°F (conventional) or 325°F (convection). Set the rack in the middle of the oven.

2. Line a sheet pan with parchment or a nonstick silicone baking mat.

3. Set out the ingredients.

• Measure the meringue ingredients into two separate bowls and set aside.

• Measure the dry ingredients into a separate bowl and whisk for 10 seconds to blend. Set aside.

4. In the bowl of a standing mixer fitted with the wire whip attachment, whip the egg whites on high speed until stiff peaks form, 1 to 2 minutes.

5. With the mixer still on high speed, slowly add the sugar and whip for 15 seconds to incorporate. Reduce the mixer speed to medium for about 15 seconds to stabilize the meringue.

6. Stop the mixer and remove the bowl. Tap the wire whip on the side of the mixer bowl to remove all the meringue. Fold the dry ingredients into the meringue in 3 additions using a rubber spatula, working gently to avoid deflating the meringue.

7. Holding a pastry bag in one hand at the halfway mark, fold the top half of the bag down to cover your hand. If it's a reusable bag fitted with a piping tip, insert the tip into the bag to prevent the meringue from dripping out when loading the batter. Scoop the meringue into the bag with the rubber spatula. If you're using a disposable bag, cut the tip off to make a hole about ½ inch in diameter.

8. Pipe the meringues onto the lined sheet pan about 1 inch apart to allow for spreading, which is usually minimal.

9. Follow the appropriate bake times listed below.

ITEM (EITHER RECIPE)	SEA LEVEL	HIGH ALTITUDE
1-inch meringues	7–9 minutes	10–12 minutes
2-inch meringues	14 minutes	20 minutes

10. The meringues are done when they appear dry and slightly browned.

11. Remove the pan from the oven and cool to room temperature, about 10 minutes on a flat, heat-resistant surface or a wire rack.

12. Once the meringues are cooled, gently slide an offset metal spatula under each one to release from the parchment. Enjoy them right away, use them to decorate a cake, or store in an airtight container at room temperature for up to 3 days.

Chocolate Meringues

It Gets Even Better: Chocolate-Filled Meringues

Try taking your meringues to the next level by filling them with chocolate. It's easier than it sounds and a great surprise for unsuspecting dessert eaters! You can use this trick with all of the meringue recipes in the book. Pipe a 2-inch dollop onto a lined sheet pan. Place about 1 to 2 teaspoons white or bittersweet chocolate pieces in the center of the meringue. Pipe an equal amount of meringue on top of the chocolate pieces to cover. Stop applying pressure and gently lift the pastry bag up to create the meringue's peak. Bake as directed.

Hazelnut Meringues

Hazelnut meringues are a little trickier to mix than other meringues because the oil in the hazelnuts breaks down the meringue rather quickly once the dry ingredients are folded in. The batter is much looser than in the vanilla or chocolate meringues. The secret to success is simply to whip the meringue to very stiff peaks and work quickly to get the meringues into the oven—the results will be wonderful! I don't recommend filling these with chocolate since they need to go into the oven without delay, but they can be dipped in ganache after they've baked and cooled.

Like any of the other meringue recipes you can always make smaller or larger meringues than the size indicated. Just adjust the baking time accordingly and watch for the cues: a golden color, a dry appearance, and (in this case) the smell of hazelnuts baking.

EQUIPMENT: standing mixer, 15-inch pastry piping bag

YIELD: twenty to thirty 1-inch meringues or twelve to fifteen 2-inch meringues

---

INGREDIENTS

Meringue

egg whites (large), 4

extra-fine granulated sugar, 6 ounces
   (¾ cup), *or 4½ ounces (½ cup + 1 table-*
   spoon) at high altitude

vanilla extract, ¼ teaspoon

Dry

confectioners' sugar, 3 ounces (¾ cup)

hazelnut powder (page 63), 2 ounces (½ cup)

unbleached all-purpose flour, 1 ounce +
   2 tablespoons (5 tablespoons)

PREPARE AHEAD OF TIME

Make the hazelnut powder (page 63). Measure 2 ounces and reserve the remainder for another use.

1. Preheat the oven to 335°F (conventional) or 325°F (convection). Set the rack in the middle of the oven.

2. Line a sheet pan with parchment or a nonstick silicone baking mat.

3. Set out the ingredients.

• Measure the meringue ingredients into three separate bowls and set aside.

• Measure the dry ingredients into a separate bowl and whisk for 10 seconds to blend. Set aside.

4. In the bowl of a standing mixer fitted with the wire whip attachment, whip the egg whites on high speed until stiff peaks form, 1 to 2 minutes.

5. With the mixer still on high speed, slowly add the sugar and whip for 15 seconds to incorporate. Add the vanilla extract and reduce the mixer speed to medium for about 15 seconds to stabilize the meringue.

6. Stop the mixer and remove the bowl. Tap the wire whip on the side of the mixer bowl to remove all the meringue. Fold the dry ingredients into the meringue in 3 additions using a rubber spatula, working gently to avoid deflating the meringue.

7. Holding a pastry bag in one hand at the halfway mark, fold the top half of the bag down to cover your hand. If it's a reusable bag fitted with a piping tip, insert the tip into the bag to prevent the meringue from dripping out when loading the batter. Scoop the meringue into the bag with the rubber spatula. If you're using a disposable bag, cut the tip off to make a hole about ½ inch in diameter.

8. Pipe the meringues onto the lined sheet pan about 1 inch apart to allow for spreading, which is usually minimal.

9. Follow the appropriate bake times listed below.

ITEM (EITHER RECIPE)	SEA LEVEL	HIGH ALTITUDE
1-inch meringues	7–9 minutes	10–12 minutes
2-inch meringues	14 minutes	20 minutes

10. The meringues are done when they appear dry and slightly browned.

11. Remove the pan from the oven and cool to room temperature, about 10 minutes on a flat, heat-resistant surface or a wire rack.

12. Once the meringues are cooled, gently slide an offset metal spatula under each one to release from the parchment. Enjoy them right away, use them to decorate a cake, or store in an airtight container at room temperature for up to 3 days.

Hazelnut Meringues

Lemon-Chocolate Meringues

A friend of mine once requested a cake with chocolate and lemon flavors. I never thought it would taste right but I was pleasantly surprised when I tried it. Lemon and chocolate work very well together. Since then I've always looked for unlikely ways to pair them together again. Meringue is a great place for these flavors to dance together because they're not competing with a long list of other ingredients. Here the bright flavor of the lemon zest and the depth of chocolate come together to make something totally different.

EQUIPMENT: standing mixer, 15-inch pastry piping bag

YIELD: twenty to thirty 1-inch meringues or twelve to fifteen 2-inch meringues

INGREDIENTS
Meringue

egg whites (large), 4

extra-fine granulated sugar, 6 ounces (¾ cup), *or 4½ ounces (½ cup + 1 tablespoon) at high altitude*

vanilla extract, ¼ teaspoon

Dry Ingredients

confectioners' sugar, 3 ounces (¾ cup)

60% bittersweet chocolate pistoles, 1 ounce

unbleached all-purpose flour, 3 tablespoons

potato starch, 2 tablespoons

vanilla powder, 1½ teaspoons

lemon zest, 1 teaspoon

PREPARE AHEAD OF TIME

Zest the lemon with a rasp or mince the lemon zest with a chef's knife. Set aside.

1. Preheat the oven to 335°F (conventional) or 325°F (convection). Set the rack in the middle of the oven.

2. Line a sheet pan with parchment or a nonstick silicone baking mat.

3. Set out the ingredients.

• Measure the meringue ingredients into three separate bowls and set aside.

• Measure the dry ingredients into the bowl of a food processor. Pulse 2 or 3 times for 3 seconds each to break the bittersweet chocolate into ¼-inch pieces.

4. In the bowl of a standing mixer fitted with the wire whip attachment, whip the egg whites on high speed until stiff peaks form, 1 to 2 minutes.

5. With the mixer still on high speed, slowly add the sugar and whip for 15 seconds to incorporate. Add the vanilla extract and reduce the mixer speed to medium for about 15 seconds to stabilize the meringue.

6. Stop the mixer and remove the bowl. Tap the wire whip on the side of the mixer bowl to remove all the meringue. Fold the dry ingredients into the meringue in 3 additions using a rubber spatula, working gently to avoid deflating the meringue.

7. Holding a pastry bag in one hand at the halfway mark, fold the top half of the bag down to cover your hand. If it's a reusable bag fitted with a piping tip, insert the tip into the bag to prevent the meringue from dripping out when loading the batter. Scoop the meringue into the bag with the rubber spatula. If you're using a disposable bag, cut the tip off to make a hole about ½ inch in diameter.

8. Pipe the meringues onto the lined sheet pan about 1 inch apart to allow for spreading, which is usually minimal.

9. Follow the appropriate bake times listed below.

ITEM (EITHER RECIPE)	SEA LEVEL	HIGH ALTITUDE
1-inch meringues	7–9 minutes	10–12 minutes
2-inch meringues	10–14 minutes	20 minutes

10. The meringues are done when they appear dry and slightly browned.

11. Remove the pan from the oven and cool to room temperature, about 10 minutes on a flat, heat-resistant surface or a wire rack.

12. Once the meringues are cooled, gently slide an offset metal spatula under each one to release from the parchment. Enjoy them right away, use them to decorate a cake, or store in an airtight container at room temperature for up to 3 days.

Cake Assembly

Never worry about whether your cake looks perfect or not. Cakes that look homemade always get respect.

When I first tried to assemble a cake I was really worried that it would look horrible. Relax. Putting a cake together is fun. And remember, it's just a cake. No one is going to refuse a serving if it looks a little odd.

If there's a bakery near you, go on a field trip and watch them in action. Watching someone do it in person is really the best way to get the feel for how to assemble a cake. Observe how the decorators work with the cake turntable, how they hold their spatulas, and the consistency of their buttercream. Don't be intimidated by how quickly they work, just focus on their movements. I took a class on cake decorating, which taught me a lot, but I also picked up a good deal by watching the pros.

The following step-by-step guide covers the basics of assembly.

CLEAN THE SPONGE

A layer cake is made up of three components: the sponge, the filling, and the buttercream. Before beginning assembly of a layer cake, most of the time the sponge has to be cleaned— especially if it's yellow butter cake. Trimming helps to level the cake, prepares the sponge for syrup, and makes it uniform in color. All of this improves the professional image of the cake when it's cut and served.

Usually all that is required is lightly trimming off the browned parts on the outer surface of the cake with a serrated knife. The browned parts are sugars in the batter that caramelized due to their exposure to hot oven air and hot metal pans during baking. Sugars in the batter darken during the baking process. Lightly browned parts are not a sign that the cake is burned, but very dark brown and blackened portions are. By all means avoid using a cake sponge that is overbaked or burned.

If you've baked ahead of time, remove the plastic from the cake and look for metal shavings that may have come loose from lightweight cake pans in depanning. Drape the plastic over the cake turntable to use as a drop cloth for crumbs. Using very little pressure and keeping the blade slightly angled away from the cake, cut off all brown parts on the top, bottom, and sides of the cake. Any hardened parts on the cake edges, particularly the top perimeter, or crown, should be gently sawed away with the serrated knife. Discard the crumbs.

SLICE INTO LAYERS

Using the serrated knife, gently slice horizontally, parallel to the countertop. I've tried many of the gadgets and methods recommended for easy cake leveling, including dental floss, wire cutters, and cake saws. In the end, I find the serrated knife to be the quickest and most effective tool for the job. It's also versatile and can be used for other jobs in your kitchen. One tip is to get a knife that's longer than the diameter of the cake you want to slice.

Each 9-x-2-inch cake should yield two layers, each measuring ½- to ¾-inch high. Use a sawing motion as you slice through the cake from one side to the other. It takes practice to slice the cake evenly. It's easier for me to just move through the cake rather than to move the cake around on the turntable, but I've seen it done both ways.

Rest assured that while a layer may appear shallow and unimpressive on its own, when it's combined with layers of buttercream, filling, and more cake, the height will add up.

Handle with Care

Try not to touch the cake layers once they're cut. Cake warms up quickly and can break easily if it's grabbed with the fingers. Support the layers with cardboard cake circles when applying a flavoring syrup or placing them onto the cake.

Slice cake round into layers   Set aside layers not used   Dab on flavoring syrup

Apply buttercream, about 1 cup   Spread buttercream with a spatula

ASSEMBLE THE LAYERS

Begin assembly with the base layer of cake. Apply a generous amount of flavored sugar syrup to the entire surface of the cake using a 1- or 2-inch pastry brush, using a dabbing motion rather than a painting motion. The painting stroke drags the brush across the cake which rakes off crumbs and can break the edge of the cake.

Check the consistency of the buttercream each time you scoop it out of the mixer. It's best to use freshly made, thoroughly whipped buttercream that gives no resistance to the offset spatula when spreading it onto the cake. But even freshly made buttercream can settle, so whip on high speed for 5 to 10 seconds to lighten it up before scooping any out.

Scoop about 1 cup of buttercream onto the base layer. Using a metal offset spatula, spread the buttercream onto the cake in an even layer. I like to keep the spatula at a slight (10 to 15°) angle with the tip in the center of the cake as I turn the cake

layer on the turntable. Keep the spatula relatively still and let the buttercream glide across the cake layer to its edges. If you'll be using a wet filling such as lemon curd or sugared strawberries, try to create a wall around the edge to hold the liquid.

Holding a cardboard cake circle supporting another trimmed layer, dab the syrup on with the pastry brush. Invert the layer onto the cake so the moistened side comes in contact with the buttercream. If the cake has fruit or toasted nuts between the layers, then it's best to sandwich them in buttercream. Spread buttercream on the layer held in your hand and invert that side onto the cake so the buttercream will come directly in contact with the fruit or toasted nuts. Sandwiching solid objects between layers of buttercream eliminates gaps and air pockets that dry out the cake.

Repeat the steps until you have three or four layers of cake. Anything larger might be a little hard to handle later on.

Carefully line up the layers

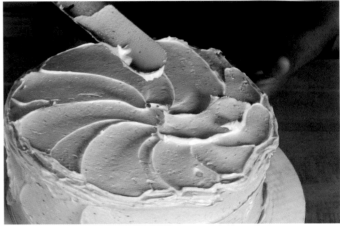

Begin crumb coat with protruding buttercream

Coating

Apply the final coat of buttercream

Set the cake in place, slide spatula between the cake and the cake circle

Slightly lift the cake away off the circle and remove the circle

Lower the cake to the platter; press the spatula against the platter when removing

APPLY THE CRUMB COAT

Next apply a crumb coat, a thin layer of buttercream that will trap the crumbs against the cake. Usually I smooth out the buttercream that oozes out the sides of the cake, then scoop ¼ – ½ cup on top of the cake, if necessary, and work that around. Less is more when it comes to the crumb coat. Refrigerate the cake for 5 to 10 minutes to let the buttercream set.

APPLY THE FINAL COAT OF BUTTERCREAM

Applying the second and final coat of buttercream is the time when you can relax and have fun. You can call in the cavalry to help you decorate or add your own signature look to the cake, so don't hold back. My preference is for a casual, homemade look. It's fast, easy, and lets a cake be a cake. If you prefer something more elaborate and advanced with piped borders, the Italian Meringue Buttercream (page 151) is suitable for making those designs.

TRANSFER TO A CAKE PLATTER

Position the frosted cake on the cardboard circle over a cake platter. Insert an offset spatula between the cake and the cardboard. Gently lift the cake about 1 inch off the cardboard and rotate the circle away from the cake (the cake stays put, the cardboard moves). Lower the cake onto the platter once the cardboard circle has been removed. Press the spatula firmly against the platter, taking pressure off the cake, to remove it.

It's Your Turn

It's important to follow the recipes closely a few times, but once you understand what's going on, have fun and innovate. Assemble a new cake with components from different recipes, or, when you're up to it, change a recipe and take ownership. It's very exciting and entirely possible to make up a new recipe. When you do, let me know. I would love to hear about it.

DECORATING WITH EASE

My style of decorating is all natural and without a lot of fuss. I love to accent a cake with elements that are already part of the cake. I'll use lemon zest for a lemon cake, candied almonds for an almond cake, cocoa powder or dots of chocolate for a chocolate cake. Anything that gives a hint of the flavor in the cake is enough for me.

Writing with Chocolate

Writing inscriptions with melted chocolate is an elegant way to personalize your efforts. Anyone with neat penmanship will be able to write well with a little practice. It's best to write on a cake that is cold, so place your finished cake in the fridge for at least 10 minutes before writing.

1. Melt ¼ cup of chocolate in a double boiler.
2. Fold a parchment triangle as shown.
3. Pour the melted chocolate into the cone and fold down the top of the cone.
4. Carefully cut off the tip of the triangle and practice a few strokes to read how the chocolate is flowing.
5. Carefully holding the triangle in place over the cake, begin writing the inscription.

The keys to writing successfully are to make the cone correctly, keep the chocolate well heated so it flows easily, and apply light but consistent pressure to the cone as you write. The chocolate shouldn't burn you through the parchment paper, but it will need to be very warm to flow easily.

After you've filled the parchment cone and snipped off the tip, squeeze out a test line to check the consistency and the breadth of the flow. Begin inscribing by bringing the parchment cone within millimeters of the cake's surface and squeeze the cone lightly, allowing the chocolate to pool slightly underneath the tip of the cone. Once the chocolate begins to flow, raise the tip away from the cake by about 2 inches and move steadily to make the pattern or letters of the inscription. Loopy letters look good on a cake, so don't be afraid to exaggerate a bit. When you need to stop the inscription or design, stop squeezing the cone and lower it to rest within millimeters of the cake. Release all your pressure on the cone and when the flow of chocolate stops, move the cone away from the cake to prevent any drips.

If you run into a problem while writing and have a few unsightly drips of chocolate on your cake, refrigerate the cake for 5 minutes to solidify the chocolate. Take a sharp paring knife and gently lift the drips off of the cake.

ADDITIONAL ACCENTS

The ingredients and recipes in this section—whether folded into batter, brushed onto pound cake, mixed into buttercream, or used as decorative flourishes—will add color, texture, and flavor to your creations. While suggestions are provided for particularly good pairings, these elements can be combined in any number of ways. Be creative, and enjoy exploring the possibilities!

Citrus
Fruit

Citrus fruits are natural flavor enhancers, and working their essential parts into a cake is not difficult. Zesting and segmenting are two common techniques that often go hand in hand.

Zesting

Rasps or plane zesters do a good job at taking only the flavorful part of the citrus peel. I usually want a little more crunch in my zest so I like to use a traditional zester that yields long strips of zest.

Zesting is easy to get the hang of, just don't press too hard and go too deep. Stay shallow to get the most flavorful, oil-rich outer layer. If you go deep you'll hit the bitter white part of the rind. No matter what tool you're using for zesting, be careful! They're all extremely sharp and they'll take off your skin very easily. I've had a few gnarly mishaps with zesters.

Segmenting

Segmenting takes some time to master but it's well worth the effort. It allows you to capture the juiciest part of the fruit for your baking and adds an engaging visual effect. Each segment is comprised of bunches and bunches of individual vesicles. The tiny vesicles of fruit are perfect little pouches that hold the fruit's juice and prevent the batter or buttercream from becoming watery.

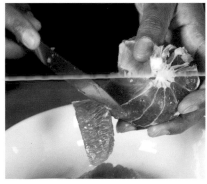

1. Using a sharp paring knife, cut the peel down to the juicy flesh of each fruit.

2. Slide the blade of the paring knife just inside the lines of the white membranes that divide the segments.

3. When the knife is at the center, gently twist the blade toward the segment you're removing and it will come free.

4. Peel the segment away from the fruit and continue separating the others from the membrane.

Toasted Almonds

These are perfect for decorating the sides or tops of cakes and cupcakes. Toasting them with just a touch of Sugar Syrup adds a delicate crunch that contrasts nicely with the softness of cake or buttercream. The first "birthday" cake I ever made featured toasted almonds pressed into orange buttercream over a rich yellow cake. It was an easy decoration, but that didn't make it any less special. That cake sums up everything I love about cakes: flavor, texture, and simplicity.

Watch your timing very carefully when toasting nuts. They have a tendency to look underdone when really they're just right. My rule is to take them out when the nuts around the edge of the sheet pan appear brown just around the edges. The recommended baking time is 5 minutes, and you'll probably never need to bake them for longer than 7 minutes.

EQUIPMENT: mixing bowl

YIELD: 1 cup

Ingredients

sliced almonds, 4½ ounces (1 cup)
Sugar Syrup (page 210), ¼ cup

1. Preheat the oven to 350°F (conventional) or 335°F (convection). Set the rack in the middle of the oven.

2. Line a sheet pan with parchment and spray with a nonstick spray if you want the nuts to release more easily from the parchment after baking.

3. Combine the nuts and Sugar Syrup in a large bowl and toss well with a rubber spatula for about 1 minute, or until the almonds are thoroughly coated with the Sugar Syrup. Using slightly exaggerated folding motions works well.

4. Spread the sugar-coated nuts in an even layer on the parchment-lined sheet pan. Bake for 4 minutes.

5. Check for browning almonds around the sides of the sheet pan. It may be necessary to stir the nuts to redistribute them if there are spots where the nuts aren't browning at all. If you've had to stir them, bake for 2 to 3 minutes longer.

6. When the nuts are slightly browned on the edges remove the sheet pan from the oven and set it on a heat-resistant surface or wire rack to cool.

7. Transfer the cooled nuts to a bowl for immediate use or label, date, and store in an airtight container at room temperature.

Toasted Coconut

There is nothing worse than baking a beautiful cake from scratch only to accent it with something that has a decidedly manufactured look or taste. Commercially sweetened coconut is one of those common accompaniments that gets pushed to the side of the plate and stays there. I never enjoyed coconut until we began toasting unsweetened coconut with our own Sugar Syrup. The difference is astounding and helped me understand why people love coconut so much. Pair toasted coconut with Coconut Buttercream as a filling between layers, or use it as an accent decor on the outside of the cake. Coconut also pairs well Yellow Butter Cake with Lemon Curd filling.

Toasting coconut correctly requires careful attention, as it turns from not baked to hopelessly burned within seconds. Timing is critical, so please turn on the oven light, grab a chair, and watch this closely the first time it's baked. With the oven set at 350°F you'll probably never need to bake the coconut for longer than 7 minutes.

EQUIPMENT: mixing bowl

YIELD: 1 cup

Ingredients

unsweetened coconut flakes, 4 ounces (1 cup)
Sugar Syrup (page 210), ¼ cup

1. Preheat the oven to 350°F (conventional) or 335°F (convection). Set the rack in the middle of the oven.

2. Line a sheet pan with parchment and spray with a nonstick spray if you want the coconut to release more easily from the parchment after baking.

3. Combine the coconut and Sugar Syrup in a large bowl and toss well with a rubber spatula for about 1 minute, or until the coconut is thoroughly covered with the Sugar Syrup. Using slightly exaggerated folding motions works well.

4. Spread the sugar-coated coconut in an even layer on the parchment-lined sheet pan. Bake for 4 minutes.

5. Check for browning coconut around the sides of the sheet pan. It may be necessary to stir the coconut to redistribute it if there are spots where the coconut isn't browning at all. If you've had to stir them, bake for 2 to 3 minutes longer.

6. When the coconut is slightly browned on the edges remove the sheet pan from the oven and set it on a heat-resistant surface or wire rack to cool.

7. Transfer the cooled coconut to a bowl for immediate use or label, date, and store in an airtight container at room temperature.

Sugar Syrup

I don't like using a simple syrup, a one-to-one ratio of sugar to water, because it's too thin. Whether it's used for brushing onto cake layers or sweetening toasted nuts, simple syrup makes the components a little too wet. This sugar syrup has almost double the amount of sugar.

EQUIPMENT: 2-quart, heavy-bottomed saucepan

YIELD: 1½ cups

Ingredients

extra-fine granulated sugar, 16 ounces (2 cups)

water, 1¼ cups

Combine the sugar and water in a 2-quart, heavy-bottomed saucepan and stir thoroughly. Bring the mixture to a light simmer over medium-high heat to dissolve the sugar. Do not bring to a rolling boil. Immediately remove the mixture from the heat and set aside to cool completely. Label, date, and refrigerate in an airtight container.

VARIATIONS

You can flavor this syrup with liqueurs of your choice, using 1 to 2 tablespoons per ½ cup of syrup. For alcohol-free variations, cook the syrup with up to 2 tablespoons of orange, lemon, or lime zest.

Home-Brewed Espresso Syrup

Put the pedal to the metal for any coffee-flavored cake with a heavy soaking of an espresso syrup. The steps below imitate the espresso machine process but at a very basic level. If you don't have an espresso machine at home, now you can make espresso—this method will work without fail.

EQUIPMENT: electric coffee grinder, fine-mesh sieve, mixing bowl

YIELD: about ½ cup

Ingredients

cold water, 1 cup

espresso beans, ¼ cup

Sugar Syrup (facing page), ½ cup

1. Bring the water to a boil.

2. Meanwhile, grind the espresso beans to the finest grain possible, about a full minute, and place the ground espresso into a fine-mesh sieve set over a bowl and level with your finger.

3. Slowly drizzle the boiling water over the ground espresso in a circular motion. Notice the bubbles that come off the grinds and the froth in the middle—that's the signal that we're taking the good flavor from the beans and not the bitterness. Keep drizzling the water slowly around the bowl of the strainer until the bubbles disappear, about 30 seconds.

4. Remove the sieve and add the sugar syrup. Allow to cool to room temperature, then label, date, and refrigerate in an airtight container.

Raspberry Puree

This is a natural way to harness the powerful flavor of raspberries. It's also a great way to dye buttercream pink!

EQUIPMENT: 2-quart, heavy-bottomed saucepan, fine-mesh sieve, mixing bowl

YIELD: about 2 cups

Ingredients

frozen raspberries, thawed, 12 to 16 ounces
extra-fine granulated sugar, 4 ounces (½ cup)

1. Thaw a package of frozen raspberries in the bag. Do not strain the juice.

2. Combine the raspberries and their juice with the sugar in a 2-quart, heavy-bottomed saucepan. Gently bring the mixture to a simmer over medium heat and promptly remove from the heat.

3. Scrape the puree from the bowl using a rubber spatula and carefully strain through a fine-mesh sieve set over a large bowl. Try to capture all of the raspberry seeds in the strainer.

4. Scrape the underside of the strainer—a lot of great puree won't drop into the bowl without some help.

5. Transfer the puree to an airtight container. Label, date, and store it in the refrigerator for up to 10 days.

Raspberry Puree being added to Sugar Syrup

Soured Dried Cherries

Slightly soured, meaty, plump, and dark, these reconstituted cherries are great substitutes when fresh cherries aren't available. If it's cherry season and you can tolerate pitting them, fresh cherries will taste even better. Use the reserved liquid as a soaking syrup for whatever cake you're pairing with the cherries to bring out even more cherry flavor.

EQUIPMENT: 2-quart, heavy-bottomed saucepan, fine-mesh sieve

YIELD: 2 cups (enough for one 9-inch-round cake)

Ingredients

dried cherries, or pitted fresh cherries,
   8 ounces
extra-fine granulated sugar, 4 ounces (½ cup)
apple cider vinegar, ¼ cup

1. Combine the ingredients in a 2-quart, heavy-bottomed sauce-pan. Bring to simmer over medium heat, then remove from the heat and let the cherries steep in the syrup for 30 minutes.

2. Allow to cool to room temperature, then transfer to an airtight container. Label, date, and refrigerate.

3. Strain the cherries prior to use, reserving the liquid for another use.

Sugared Strawberries

I can remember my Grandma Sallie telling me that the best way to eat strawberries was to cut them up, put some sugar on them, and leave them in the refrigerator overnight. For best results, use fresh, ripe strawberries when they're in season, but frozen berries can be substituted in a pinch. Sugared Strawberries can be layered with Yellow or Chocolate Butter Cake, or any No-Mixer Cake. When paired with "LCD" Vanilla Pound Cake and Whipped Cream, they make for an absolutely delicious strawberry shortcake.

EQUIPMENT: colander, mixing bowl

YIELD: about 2 cups

Ingredients

fresh strawberries, or frozen strawberries,
  thawed, 2 pints

extra-fine granulated sugar, 4 ounces (½ cup)

1. Wash the berries in a colander and let them drain.

2. Hull (cut the leafy tops off) the berries and quarter them with a paring knife.

3. Combine the berries and sugar in a large bowl and toss well with a rubber spatula for about 30 seconds, or until the berries are thoroughly coated with the sugar.

4. Refrigerate the berries for 4 to 12 hours—the longer the better.

5. Strain the liquid and reserve for another use. (It tastes terrific in fresh-squeezed lemonade.)

6. Use the berries right away or transfer the berries to an airtight container. Label, date, and store in the refrigerator for up to 5 days.

"LCD" Vanilla Pound Cake with Whipped Cream and Sugared Strawberries

Conversion Charts

ALL-PURPOSE FLOUR

When I teach baking classes at CakeLove and on the road, everyone tells me they scoop and level. Everyone. As you'll notice when reading this book, I believe it's critical to weigh certain ingredients for successful baking. Anytime a recipe calls for more than 2 tablespoons of one of the ingredients listed below, I'll weigh it. I didn't want to weigh ingredients when I started baking, but everyone who tasted the cakes immediately noticed the difference.

I know it's really difficult to break old habits, but the scoop-and-level method is not accurate. Dry ingredients—especially flour—compress too easily into a cup measure for scooping and leveling to be reliable. The solution is to measure with a scale (see page 25).

In addition, please note that the most accurate method for measuring flour is to weigh it after sifting. I sift flour into a bowl placed on a scale whenever I bake at CakeLove. If I don't have a scale I sift the flour into a bowl and very delicately scoop and level into a cup measure without packing it down.

WEIGHT (MASS)	VOLUME
1 ounce	3 tablespoons
2 ounces	¼ cup + 2 tablespoons
3 ounces	½ cup + 1 tablespoon
4 ounces	¾ cup + ½ teaspoon
5 ounces	1 cup
6 ounces	1 cup + 1 tablespoon
7 ounces	1¼ cups + 2 tablespoons
8 ounces	1½ cups + 1 tablespoon
9 ounces	1¾ cups + ½ teaspoon
10 ounces	2 cups
11 ounces	2 cups + 1 tablespoon
12 ounces	2¼ cups + 2 tablespoons
12½ ounces	2½ cups
13 ounces	2½ cups + 1 tablespoon
13½ ounces	2½ cups + 3 tablespoons
14 ounces	2¾ cups + ½ teaspoon
14½ ounces	2¾ cups + 1 tablespoon +1 teaspoon
15 ounces	3 cups

EXTRA-FINE GRANULATED SUGAR

Extra-fine granulated sugar is the standard sugar used in this book. According to the American Sugar Council, it weighs in at 7.9 ounces per cup, but I round up to 8 ounces for simplicity. Standard table sugar, or typical granulated sugar, weighs 7 ounces per cup. It has a larger crystal than extra-fine granulated, so less mass fits into a one-cup measure.

WEIGHT (MASS)	VOLUME
1 ounce	2 tablespoons
2 ounces	¼ cup
3 ounces	6 tablespoons
4 ounces	½ cup
5 ounces	½ cup + 2 tablespoons
6 ounces	¾ cup
7 ounces	¾ cup + 2 tablespoons
8 ounces	1 cup
12 ounces	1½ cups
16 ounces	2 cups
20 ounces	2½ cups
24 ounces	3 cups

OTHER INGREDIENTS

INGREDIENT	WEIGHT (MASS)	VOLUME
almonds (slivered)	4½ ounces	1 cup
butter	4 ounces	8 tablespoons (1 stick)
chocolate pistoles	10 ounces	1 cup
confectioners' sugar	4¼ ounces	1 cup
cocoa powder	1 ounce	¼ cup
hazelnuts (whole)	5 ounces	1 cup
walnuts (whole)	3½–4 ounces	1 cup

LIQUID MEASUREMENT EQUIVALENTS

Use volume measurements for liquid ingredients like milk, half-and-half, sour cream, heavy cream, fruit juices, and liqueurs.

You don't have to be a math whiz to bake well, but it helps to understand the mathematical relationships of common units of measure.

3 teaspoons	=	1 tablespoon
4 tablespoons	=	¼ cup (2 fluid ounces)
8 tablespoons	=	½ cup (4 fluid ounces)
16 tablespoons	=	1 cup (8 fluid ounces)
2 cups	=	1 pint (16 fluid ounces)
4 cups	=	1 quart

References

Beranbaum, Rose Levy. **The Cake Bible.** New York: William Morrow and Company, 1988.

Cook's Illustrated Magazine, Editors of. **Baking Illustrated.** New York: America's Test Kitchen, 2004.

Daley, Regan. **In the Sweet Kitchen.** New York: Artisan, 2001.

Gand, Gale, Rick Tramonto, and Julia Moskin. **Butter Sugar Flour Eggs.** New York: Clarkson Potter, 1999.

Greenspan, Dorie. **Baking with Julia.** New York: William Morrow and Company, 1996.

Healy, Bruce. **The Art of the Cake.** New York: William Morrow and Company, 1999.

Malgieri, Nick. **How to Bake.** New York: HarperCollins, 1995.

McGee, Harold. **On Food and Cooking.** New York: Scribner, 2004.

Ortiz, Elisabeth Lambert. **The Encyclopedia of Herbs, Spices and Flavorings.** London: Dorling Kindersley, 1992.

Resources

La Cuisine (specialty baker ware)
323 Cameron Street
Alexandria, VA 22314
(800) 521-1176
www.lacuisineus.com

India Tree (specialty sugars)
1421 Elliott Avenue West
Seattle, WA 98119
(800) 369-4848
www.indiatree.com

Fran's Cake & Candy (small tools)
10396 Willard Way
Fairfax, VA 22030
(703) 352-1471

Frontier Natural Products Co-op (spices)
PO Box 299
3021 78th Street
Norway, IA 52318
(800) 669-3275
www.frontiercoop.com

New York Cake Supplies (small tools)
56 West 22nd Street
New York, NY 10010
(800) 942-2539
www.nycake.com

Acknowledgments

A tremendous set of hugs, kisses, and blessings goes to my family. Without their support from the beginning, I would not have had the courage and faith to carry out this mission. I especially want to thank my parents for their constant support; my sisters, Lenora and Elizabeth, for their editorial help and visual guidance with this book and many other projects related to CakeLove; and Yvette and Howard for offering their apartment as a sanctuary for writing, and also for the banter that makes conversations fun.

I want to thank my partner, Pam Young, for her support and patience throughout this process.

I want to thank everyone that I'm lucky enough to work with at CakeLove and LoveCafe. Without their tireless efforts and total kick-butt attitude, this book (and my dream for growing CakeLove) would not be possible.

I would especially like to thank several members of my staff who have been with me through thick and thin—in the late nights and wee hours of the morning—and have offered support, jokes, and laughs: Cynthia Gooding, Kim Lamore, Christine Eigenbrode, Jorge Prudencio, Jasmin Hedgpeth, Chris Spinosa, Sheila Vargas, and Jackie Bell.

Thank you to Mary Meyers for non-stop support and carrying extra-heavy loads of everything when I've needed the extra help.

Thank you to Joanna Goode for early rounds of copyediting.

Thank you to Ellice Perez for giving me the structure that enabled me to focus on this book.

Thank you to Porche Lovely for testing my recipes at high altitude.

Thank you to Renée Comet and everyone at Comet Photography for the beautiful pictures that do a better job than I can of telling the story of how to bake cakes from scratch.

Thank you to the folks at Stewart, Tabori & Chang—particularly Jennifer Levesque, Kate Norment, and Chris Gardner—for working endlessly to make a useful, practical guide for novice and experienced bakers.

Thanks to my agent, Ian Kleinert, for helping me understand and wade through the process of my first book.

There is also a very long list of friends who have helped me along the way and I'm afraid that I'll forget someone who has been there for me, but I do want to mention some of those who have helped me up when I've fallen, lent a helping hand when I needed it, or just gone out of their way to visit: Kit Miller, Emily McCarthy, Brian Monnin, Margaret Braun, Deepti Sethi, David Herbruck, Bruce Durbin, Sarah Ingersoll, Neil Barret, Judy Weinraub, and Jill Wesley.

Thank you to the Food Network for giving me a platform to bring my message to the world.

And, of course, thanks to all of the customers who visit CakeLove and LoveCafe for birthday cakes, cupcakes, and more. Your enthusiasm keeps this engine going—thank you for believing in small businesses and for your continued support.

Index

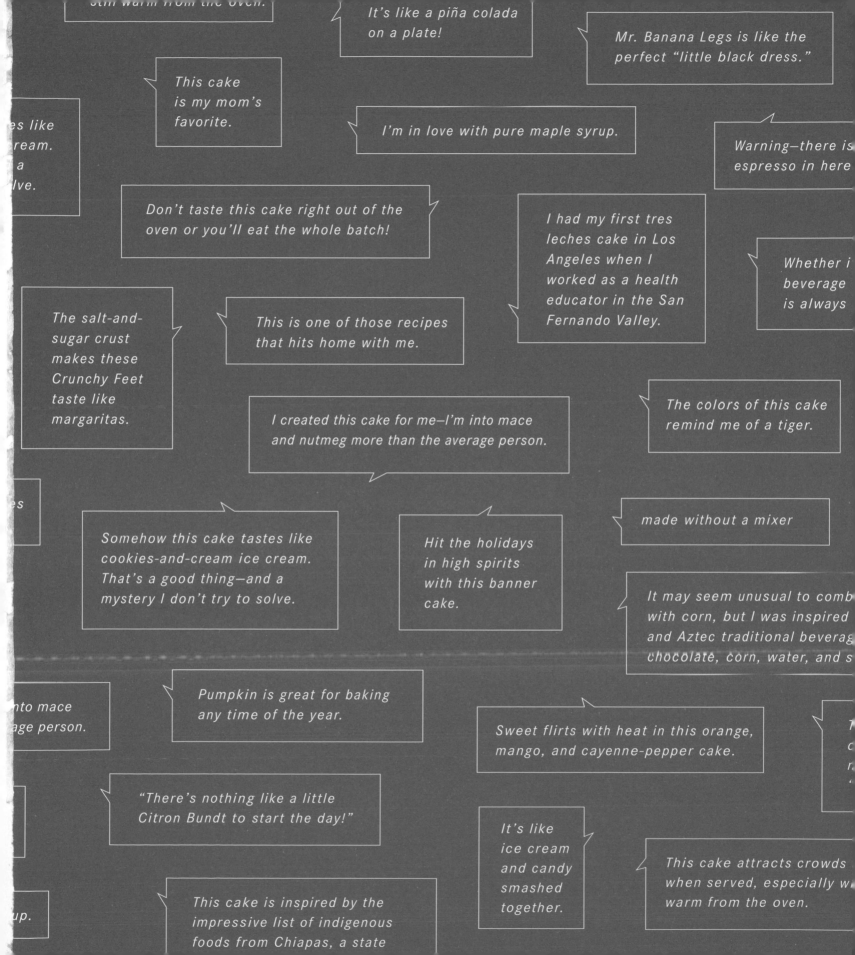